IOWA'S RECORD SETTING GOVERNOR

THE TERRY BRANSTAD STORY

IOWA'S RECORD SETTING GOVERNOR

THE TERRY BRANSTAD STORY

MIKE CHAPMAN

Business Publications Corporation Inc.

Iowa's Record Setting Governor: The Terry Branstad Story is published by Business Publications Corporation Inc., an Iowa corporation.

Leland Iowa
Words and Music by John J. Coinman.

ISBN-13: 978-0-9965213-1-4
Library of Congress Control Number: 2015955798

Business Publications Corporation Inc.
The Depot at Fourth
100 4th Street
Des Moines, Iowa 50309
(515) 288-3336

DEDICATION:

To all Iowans with the courage to follow their dreams.

Acknowledgements

A book of this scope is a tremendous undertaking, and I am deeply appreciative of the support I received. First and foremost on the list of those who assisted me is Mike Reese, who has a degree in history from Iowa State University and is owner of the Atlas Media company in Des Moines. Mike offered his time and energy by researching the various political campaigns of Governor Branstad, and his enthusiasm for the project was an added plus along the way.

Also high on the list is Ruth Leibrand of the Mansion Museum in Forest City, who was eager to assist in any way she could. Three times I journeyed up to Forest City to conduct research in the beautiful facility and to chat with her and others about the formative years of Terry Branstad. Ruth has been indefatigable in her efforts to keep alive the history of the area. She introduced me to several other people, including Carol Whiteis and Riley Lewis, who were willing to share stories of the governor's family and early years. The Branstad room is very well maintained, and I encourage anyone interested in the governor's story to visit the museum.

Margaret Hough has worked with Terry Branstad as a key staff member for over two decades, both in his role as governor and during his years as president of Des Moines University. She is a tireless, energetic worker who takes great pride in helping keep the governor's schedule on track and his legacy intact. Her help on this project was indispensable.

I conducted over thirty interviews during the past eighteen months with, among others, associates and longtime acquaintances of the governor, and read hundreds of news articles and several books. Chris Branstad gave my wife and me a tour of Terrace Hill and shared some wonderful stories. Wanting to learn more about what he is like to work for, I also talked to a number of staff people who have served the governor and his family. While most of these comments are not actually included in the book, they were important to me in my quest to understand what type of employer and leader he is. Frankly, everyone I contacted was eager to talk about the career of America's longest serving governor, and their respect for him as both a politician and a person was apparent and unforced. He is deeply admired by all I talked to.

Of course, I must thank Terry Branstad for being so open with me in all our conversations. He takes tremendous pride in the remarkable story of this state and is fully aware that his role in its history is secure. Yet he remains remarkably modest about all of his accomplishments and is quick to share the successes with his staff and supporters.

Lastly, I am deeply appreciative of the support of my wife, Bev, during this process. She was encouraging every step of the way and was willing to listen to my long-winded stories and share in my adventures as I chased down sources of information and waded through mounds of research. I could not have written this book without her assistance.

Contents

Introduction

Although I was a newspaperman for 35 years, have authored 27 books to date, and created two magazines from scratch, this project was one of the most challenging of my career. Many of my books are biographies, and that is the type of work that I enjoy the most. However, a book about politics requires an extensive amount of research that deals with many complex issues and levels of detail. With those thoughts uppermost in mind, I should point out that this book is not meant to be a blow-by-blow account of the political career of Terry Branstad but, rather, an overview of a fascinating life that will hopefully provide insight into what drives him, and also inspire younger generations to work hard and dream big. Any reader hoping to find an in-depth probe into the machinations of the Iowa political scene and backroom style maneuverings may be somewhat disappointed.

My goal from the outset was to take the reader on a trip down the path traveled by an Iowan who grew up in very modest circumstances on the family farm but was fueled even as a young man by an intense desire to become a key player at the highest levels of governance. Terry Branstad wasn't propelled by a hyperactive ego or a sense of entitlement; rather, he was driven by a burning desire to make a difference in a state that he truly loves.

Through my long journalistic journey I have met many remarkable men and women – sports heroes, movie actors, business leaders, media stars and politicians. Among that group are several persons that I have been fortunate to consider friends and get to know very well. Those associations have enabled me to observe up close and personal their methods of attaining the highest levels of success. On that list is Dan Gable, considered by some to be the most successful college coach in any sport in American history, and Bob Mathias, an Olympic champion who went on to a long and distinguished career as a United States Congressman, movie actor and statesman. Gable and Mathias share many of the same qualities that carried them to the highest levels of success – two of those qualities being an unrestrained passion for their chosen field of activity and an insatiable drive to make a difference.

Terry Branstad was blessed with those same two characteristics. For over two decades, I have observed the governor from a distance, and once I began work on this book I was at first impressed and then, finally, amazed at his passion, energy and commitment to his ideals. On several occasions, I felt that his love of the State of Iowa borders on obsession ... a very healthy obsession that has benefitted millions of Iowans over the course of his long career.

Iowans and political wonks may not agree with every decision that Terry Branstad has made, or his basically conservative style of leadership, but very few people will question his work ethic or his affection for all things Iowa. His memory is tremendous, and he relishes every opportunity to reminisce about his youth in north central Iowa. He remembers the names of all of his childhood teachers, and most of his classmates. And he talks with genuine enthusiasm when he discusses their paths and successes in life.

Remarkably, in private conversations he seldom dwells on his own accomplishments. And just as remarkably for a politician, he is a great listener. He truly enjoys hearing Iowans speak about their state.

If nothing else, I hope readers of this book will come away with a deeper understanding and appreciation of the man who has grabbed the record book in a headlock and held it tight as he became the longest serving governor in not only Iowa history but American history, as well. That was my objective at the outset and was the guiding principle throughout the project.

Mike Chapman
Newton, Iowa

IOWA'S RECORD SETTING GOVERNOR

THE TERRY BRANSTAD STORY

CHAPTER ONE

Growing Up in Leland

Upon entering Leland, Iowa, today, a traveler would find no indication that it is the hometown of the longest serving governor in Iowa history. Or, for that matter, the hometown of the man who has now become the longest serving governor in all of American history!

The little berg sits quietly on Highways 69 north and 9 west, just four miles north of Forest City. On this particular crisp autumn Sunday afternoon in 2013, there is no sign of activity, save for a man mowing his yard. A traveler can pass through Leland in about thirty seconds, as there are only six streets running adjacent to the highway. What's more, there are only six streets to the east and just three to the west.

There is no active school in Leland today and just one house of worship—Our Savior's Lutheran Church—and beside it the only park, which offers a couple of swings, a colorful jungle gym, and a single tennis court. There are three businesses on the highway—Leland's Woodworks and K&C Electric, both on the east side, and Finer Cabinetry on the west side. There is a sign for Bob's Cabinetry, just a block away.

Also on the east side of the highway is Mitchell's Bar 'N' Grill, with a statue of a black pig next to the entrance. The US Post Office is a small building at 212 West Broadway, on the same side of the street as the Ted Branstad VFW Post 6161, named for Terry's cousin who served in World War II. In between the two buildings is a tiny concrete structure that once served as city hall but now is privately owned. The current city hall and community center is a block south at 316 Walnut Street.

Those passing through the town are greeted by signs on both ends of the highway that say: "Welcome to Leland – A Great Place to Call Home." The signs also proclaim that Watermelon Days are held every year, going back to 1934.

The village was named for John D. Leland, who was born in Lane County, New York, and moved to both Ohio and Illinois before coming to Forest City in 1880 to open a law firm. Leland bought a large tract of land north of Forest City and platted a village, where he set up a general store and practiced law, and occasionally even used his home for a hotel. Since he also served as the postmaster, he called the village Lelandsburg.

John Leland died on May 20, 1911, at age seventy-five. His namesake lives on, but just barely. That fact was drummed home in dramatic fashion on January 28, 2009, when one of the world's best-known movie actors showed up at Mitchell's diner. Kevin Costner and his Modern West Band tour the country from time to time, usually hitting big cities like Tampa, Des Moines, and Minneapolis. But one of their songs is about Leland, Iowa, and what life was like there many years ago, so they decided to perform there in 2009.

The song goes like this:

> "Take a walk down main street,
> have a look around.
> Now look in all the windows.
> The empty buildings in this town.
> Imagine all the people,
> Who came and had to go.
> Look for something better,
> In the dream on down the road.
> You can't spend a dime in Leland, Iowa,
> 'cause every store in town's run out of luck."

Reprinted by Permission of Hal Leonard Corporation

There's more to the song, but the point is obvious—there's not a lot going on in Leland, Iowa, these days. In the census of 2010, Leland had just 289 residents.

Today, the town's most famous citizen lives in the governor's mansion in Des Moines, but he still harbors many fond memories of life in Leland.

"It is my hometown, and it was a great place to grow up," said Terry Branstad, who was born in Leland on November 17, 1946. "It had a high school until 1945. I went to grade school there, and I still remember the names of the kids in my class."[1]

Terry and his brother, Monroe—four years younger than Terry and known as Monty—grew up on the family farm just south of town, bordering on the Winnebago River. Their father, Edward, was a handsome Norwegian Lutheran, and his mother, the former Rita Garland, was a pretty Jewish girl who was born in Burlington and spent her early years there while her father owned several stores. After he lost them all in the Great Depression, he worked for Jack Robinson in Sioux City, then moved to Lake Mills, just north of Leland, and started all over. Tenacious and determined to survive the financial calamity that had befallen him, Garland bought the entire inventory of retail stores going out of business and then sold the merchandise for bargain prices at his Lake Mills store.

Edward Branstad, who was born on March 9, 1924, was also raised on the family farm—and still owned it at the time of his death on July 26, 2013, at the age of eighty-nine. Edward graduated from Leland High School and attended Waldorf College in Forest City for a year, where he met Rita. After they were married, they settled on the family farm.

Ed and Rita raised their two sons with a strong work ethic and a belief in the promise of America. When they had to struggle to keep the farm operating during some lean years, both Ed and Rita took second jobs, driving to Albert Lea, Minnesota, with another local couple to work in a factory. They would leave Leland around 4:00 a.m. and arrive back home late in the afternoon and then start their day all over again, this time on the farm.

Working from sunup to sunset and often into the night became a Branstad family tradition in Leland and provided the foundation for a future governor's outlook on life.

"My dad's favorite saying was, 'Well, we didn't get much done today, but we will give it heck tomorrow,'" said Terry Branstad with a chuckle several months following his father's death, "and that was after we had put in a long fourteen-hour day."[2]

During the 1980s farm crisis, Ed again took a second job, this time as the county director of the Hancock County Agricultural Stabilization and Conservation Service (ASCS). It was not unusual for him to put in a full day at the office in Garner, then head home to the farm and work until midnight.

Hard work was the trait that enabled the Branstad family to survive and eventually flourish. It is also the common thread that runs through Terry Branstad's entire life and career.

"Oh, Ed and Rita were very hardworking people, and Terry was cut from the same cloth," said Ruth Leibrand, who is in charge of the archives at the Mansion Museum in Forest City. "I think everyone around here would agree to that. He knew how to work, and he learned that from his parents."[3]

Frankly, it was almost impossible for a young Branstad to do anything but put in long, hard days.

"We had a very diversified family farm operation," said Branstad. "We raised chickens, pigs, cattle, sheep; we had dairy cows and work horses in my early years. Our house was situated up on a hill, and we had to carry pails of water for the chickens. We had 144 acres, and worked another hundred acres of my grandmother's farm, which Dad called his 'east place.' My dad bought another eighty acres when I was in high school.

"When I was in sixth grade, we had over one hundred ewes. It was my responsibility to make sure that when a ewe had baby lambs, the lambs were nursing and in a pen and had heat lamps, food, and water."[4]

Education was also a family priority, and the boys learned that at an early age. Leland didn't offer a kindergarten program in those years, and Terry was put on a bus every morning by his mother to attend school in Forest City. Soon after, Leland started its own kindergarten.

"We had the same teacher in kindergarten, first, and second grades—Miss Peterson," he said. "She was great. When we came back for first grade, her name was Mrs. Ambroson, as she had gotten married in the summer."

In 2013, Branstad still remembered the names of his classmates from first grade in Leland and delighted in rattling them off: Jan Haugen, Martha Holland, Lois McLain, Tom Ambroson, and Paul Buren. When he was in the third grade, the local country schools closed, and the class was joined by Virgil Moen, Douglas Meinecke, Robert and Dennis Nath, and Harold and Marjorie Swenson.

Caring about people with whom he came in contact was a skill nurtured by the young Branstad, and would become a key ingredient of his political success. "Terry has an uncanny ability to remember people and connect faces with names," said Lyle Simpson, a prominent Des Moines attorney who played a large role in Branstad's political career. "That ability has been a big asset through the years."[5]

But there was more to life in the 1940s and '50s than just hard work and going to school. Growing up in northern Iowa gave a youngster plenty of opportunities to traverse the land and to learn to appreciate Iowa's rich heritage. The rolling terrain offered pockets of forest to explore, streams to navigate, and fields of prairie grass in which to roam.

Today, just across the highway and a short distance south of the Branstad farm, lays the Ambroson Recreation Area, a total of 119 acres that features an Iowa Fish Hatchery Program run by the Winnebago Conservation Board. The area preserves the land as it was when the Branstad boys were growing up in the 1950s, and long before.

The Winnebago River cut through the Branstad farm, and Terry, Monty, and their pals played Robin Hood in the woods, hunted pigeons with Daisy BB guns, trapped pocket gophers, and hunted raccoons, ducks, and squirrels. He even joined the Leland Fox Club when he was twelve and was given a pin to wear on his hat.

"In the winter, we'd go after foxes and jackrabbits," he said. "There would be forty to fifty men and boys, and sometimes we'd get as many as five foxes and maybe forty or fifty jackrabbits. Hans Holton and Hap Buren were the leaders and organizers of the Leland Fox Club."[6]

However, one of his biggest adventures didn't meet with the approval of his mother. A friend, Ron Holland, went into a local barbershop one day and emerged with a haircut that was rather daring, if not downright outlandish. It featured a thick strip of hair down the middle of the scalp and both sides completely bare. It was a style that was referred to as a Mohawk, after the Indian tribe featured in the famous novel *The Last of The Mohicans*, by James Fenimore Cooper. Branstad thought it was cool and decided he needed one, too.

"It was when I was in sixth grade, and my mom wasn't too pleased," he said with a smile. "Ron Holland gave me the idea for it."[7] The hair grew out quickly, and it was the last Mohawk haircut Branstad ever tried. Sadly, Holland never lived to see his friend make it into the governor's office as he was killed in a biking accident a few years later.

The future governor can quickly rattle off the names of many of the business owners—and the main law enforcement officer—in Leland during his youth. "Otto Nolte was the police chief and also the mayor," said Branstad. "We'd give him a hard time doing rather harmless stuff, and he'd chase us around a little. When TV came in during the 1950s, he sold Dumont televisions and also ran Nolte's café, where his wife was the cook. Sharon Roberts, their granddaughter, still lives in Leland."

There were two grocery stores, a grain elevator, a hatchery, three gas stations, and a bar. "Hap Buren was the barber, next to Gunderson's Grocery, and he had arrowheads and even a tomahawk," Branstad recalled.[8]

To while away the long days of summer, there were squirt guns fights, with water taken from a well in the middle of the street. Movies were a special treat for youngsters growing up in small Midwestern towns in the 1950s, and Leland was no exception. Cowboy films, often produced on very small budgets with familiar themes, and cartoons cranked out in large numbers by the various studios, were the main attractions.

"We had no movie theater, but during the summer they held free movies on a big screen that was set up in a vacant lot," he recalled.

"They would play polka music beforehand, and then we'd settle down to watch the movie. It was a big deal for the kids."[9]

Though Branstad doesn't recall the name Bob Baker, there is a chance that he saw the Forest City native in one of the older black-and-white westerns that would flash across the screen. Born Stanley Weed in Forest City on November 8, 1910, Baker's middle name was Leland, given in honor of his mother's father, John D. Leland, who had founded the village.

Stanley Leland Weed wound up in Hollywood and became a star of B-level western films in the late 1930s and early '40s, after being picked from a number of hopefuls for the spot at Universal Studios. The studio changed Weed's name to Bob Baker . . . and one of the fellows he beat out for his first starring role was Leonard Slye from Duck Run, Ohio. After losing out to the Forest City actor, Slye was subsequently picked up by Republic Pictures and changed his name to Roy Rogers!

But Terry Branstad found a local hero in Herb Thompson, who led Forest City to second place in the 1949 Iowa High School State Basketball Championships. Forest City was beaten by Ottumwa in the 1949 finals 39–27, scoring just seven points in the entire second half—all of them by Thompson. And Thompson set a new state scoring record for the entire tournament.

Thompson's impact as a state hero was captured in a column written for the University of Iowa student newspaper during his first year there. The writer was Jack Bender, who went on to spend a long career as an editorial cartoonist and eventually as the artist for the nationally syndicated *Alley Oop* comic strip.

"A four-year varsity regular at Forest City High School, Herb was selected on the all-state first team his last two seasons," wrote Bender. "During those four years the Forest City quintet embedded itself on the basketball map of Iowa. Herb comes from a high school with an enrollment of 275. Interest in basketball is so high there, however, that 50 boys turn out for the sport every year."[10]

Thompson was a three-year starter for legendary Iowa Coach Bucky O'Connor and was named the Hawkeyes' most valuable player for the 1952–53 season. "Herb Thompson was my hero as a kid," said Branstad in 2013, while riding down Interstate 80 in his SUV en route to a football game in Iowa City, where the Hawkeyes would be facing Michigan State in a Big Ten Conference game. "He was a big basketball star back home, and then at Iowa. We listened to all the games on the radio, and I can remember talking to him when I was just a kid and how impressed I was. He later had a son, Scott, who also played basketball at Iowa.

"For a small-town kid like me, Herb Thompson was like Nile Kinnick was for Adel, someone to look up to. His sister and my aunt, Helene, played girls basketball at Leland High School."[11]

After college, Thompson embarked on a long and successful coaching career. He started out in Waverly, and in 1961, he led Mason City to fourth in the state tournament, then coached for thirteen years at Moline High School in Illinois. In 1977, he left the education field and entered into real estate, where he is still active.

"I grew up in Leland and played baseball with the governor's dad," Thompson told the author in 2014. "I run into Governor Branstad here and there, and he is always so friendly. In the 1980s, Forest City held a big school reunion, and they had John Hanson, founder of Winnebago, Governor Branstad, and me on the stage. I felt really honored to be up there with those two men.

"I don't know what to make of all that hero talk, but I'm really proud to know the governor. It's unbelievable what he has accomplished."[12]

Many a Leland lad grew up with dreams of hitting the big time, just like Herb Thompson did.

"Jan Haugen had a basketball hoop in his barn, and Leland had a small gym," Branstad recalled. Pickup games were common, and the Leland lads learned the game in barns, at Steuber's Standard Station, or wherever else they could find a hoop.

In December 1955, the Branstad family journeyed to Pasadena, California, and saw the Rose Bowl parade on January 2, 1956, but not the game, where Michigan State beat UCLA 17–14. "We drove there and camped out the night before the Rose Bowl parade," said Branstad. "My brother and I slept in the car. It was a great trip."[13]

The very next year, Forest Evashevski and his gritty band of Iowa players caught the imagination of the people of the state by posting a record of 8–1 and earning the first Rose Bowl berth in school history. The game was played on January 1, 1957, and the Branstad family of Leland was among the thousands of Iowans sitting by their television sets or radios as the Hawkeyes scored a 35–19 victory over Pacific Coast champion Oregon State. Hawkeye quarterback Kenny Ploen, a native of Clinton, was voted the game's Most Valuable Player—the same honor the Big Ten Conference had accorded him earlier—and went on to become one of the biggest stars in Canadian Football League history.

Baseball was also a popular pastime and became a big part of the Branstad family's life. Ed Branstad was a member of the Leland town team, and Terry often tagged along to see his dad's games. When Terry was in eighth grade, he went to Saint Louis with Jan Haugen and his parents, Gilmer and Virgil, to see the Cardinals.

"Stan Musial was my favorite player," he said of the Cardinal legend. "But I also liked Ted Williams (of the Boston Red Sox) and, of course, Iowan Bob Feller (the Van Meter sensation who became a hall of fame player with the Cleveland Indians)."[14]

Governor Branstad attended the dedication of the Bob Feller Museum in Van Meter in 1995, and the legendary pitcher offered an invitation to him. "He said if the Indians make it to the World Series, he wanted me to come to a game in Cleveland as his guest," Branstad recalled. "I figured the chances of the Indians doing that were slim and none. But guess what—all of a sudden there they were, in the World Series, and so I took my dad to Cleveland, and we watched the fifth game of the series sitting with Bob Feller."

In the 1960s, Terry Branstad was forging an athletic career of his own in a much smaller setting. As a youth, he played pee wee and midget baseball. In 1963, Forest City High School made it all the way to the state tournament in Des Moines, providing Branstad, in tenth grade at the time, his first trip to the capital city.

He participated in both football and baseball all four years in high school and basketball for one season. In the fall of 1964, during his senior year in high school, Forest City posted a 5–3 record in football, good for second place in the North Iowa Conference. Playing in the line on offense and in the line or at linebacker on defense, Terry Branstad was named honorable mention all-conference.

"Jim Redel was our football coach, and he inspired me and my teammates by saying, 'When the going gets tough, the tough get going!'" said the Iowa governor decades later.

Redel grew up in Cedar Rapids and was a multistar athlete at Coe College, where Marv Levy, a future NFL coaching legend, was his backfield coach. Redel coached at Forest City from 1961 through 1965 and has fond memories of Terry Branstad.

"I had Terry as a freshman in my class, and he was an ideal student," said Redel in 2014. "He worked hard and always did more than he was asked to do. I think he probably learned that from his mother. He played football for me, and he was what you would call an overachiever. He studied his position and always knew what to do.

"He weighed 169 pounds and was the second biggest kid on the team," said Redel. "He was a pulling guard, and he always wanted to be a running back. So, in our game against Lake Mills, we got way ahead, and I let him carry the ball once. He cut inside, following a block, and was on his way to a touchdown when he just dropped the ball . . . for no reason. He came back to the sidelines and said he understood why he wasn't a running back."[15]

Redel moved to West Union High School in Fayette and then to Corning, where his 1971 team went 9–0 and was ranked no. 1 in the state by the *Des Moines Register*, before playoffs went into effect. He left education in 1974 to enter the sales field and now lives in Anamosa. He is proud of his relationship with his former student who now sits in the seat of power in state government.

"I'm not the least bit surprised at what Terry has done," said Redel. "I didn't know what he was going to do, but I knew he would be a success. He was a very serious young man. Every time I see him, he is so gracious and generous with his time."[16]

The spring of his senior year, the Forest City baseball team posted a 6–3 overall record and won the sectional tournament before bowing to Waverly in district play 1–0. Branstad is proud of the fact that just the year prior, Forest City only lost to Bancroft Saint John in sectional play 1–0 on the Bancroft home field, and Saint John went on to win the state tournament.

Sports would provide an important form of relaxation for Branstad the rest of his life, and he relished attending athletic events all across the state for the next five decades. Just as important, sports taught him the lifelong lessons of how to compete at the highest levels—a skill that would serve him well once he entered the rough and tumble world of politics.

CHAPTER TWO

Miss Sewick and Mr. Goldwater

There are two figures from his schoolboy days—one local and one on the national scene—who had a huge impact on the political development of Terry Branstad and, hence, the entire state of Iowa. The first was Lura Sewick, a teacher who influenced many of the young boys and girls who paraded through her classrooms.

"Miss Sewick . . . she was very strict," said Jerry Tweeten while sitting in the archive room of the Mansion Museum in Forest City on a spring day in 2014. He shook his head with a smile growing on his face. "I was in her last class, back in 1971. She was tough, but she was a great teacher. You learned a lot in her class, and you had the feeling that she really cared about her subject and about you as an individual."[17]

Lura Sewick had a lasting impression on many of her students during her forty-five-year teaching career, and that is certainly the case with Terry Branstad.

"I am fortunate because I had good teachers, really good teachers, all through school," said Terry. "Miss Sewick taught U.S. history in eighth grade at Forest City, and she spent a lot of time on the Bill of Rights and the Constitution. She also taught us about having respect for other people's rights and opinions, and about taking responsibility.

"Fred Smith taught Iowa history and civics, and was also a football, basketball, and baseball coach. I remember I did a project in his class for which I made a large notebook, full of information about Iowa. I put the word Iowa on the cover in big letters." He paused, smiling. "I got an A for it."[18]

The notebook is now on display at the Mansion Museum, along with twelve cases of other Branstad memorabilia.

Listening to him reminisce about his school days, it is obvious that Terry holds a special place in his memory bank for Lura Sewick. He fondly recalls that she had different color eyes—"one brown and one blue, I believe"—but most of all he remembers her passion for this nation and its political and civic heritage.

"Miss Sewick made it her personal goal to get people registered to vote. One of our class assignments was to attend a city council meeting and write a report on it," Branstad recalled. "I owe a great deal of my career to those two teachers, Lura Sewick and Fred Smith; they were the catalyst for my career in politics.

"We had a mock trial in Fred Smith's class. We actually held the last portion of the trial in the Winnebago County Courthouse, and I was an attorney for the plaintiff, along with Cynthia Charlson. It was a great experience for all of us."[19]

Two members of the 1965 Forest City graduating class—Terry Branstad and Cynthia Charlson—continued their education at the University of Iowa. Charlson, who goes by Cindy, selected education as a career, and after marrying John Monroe, an attorney, she wound up in Cedar Rapids, where she was a principal at several different schools before retiring.

She remembers Rita Branstad as "a very strong woman" and is not at all surprised at the successes Terry Branstad has found in the political sphere. "I could have seen it coming in fifth and sixth grade," she said. "He loves this state and is not egocentric . . . he cares about what is beyond him."[20]

As an avowed liberal, Cindy admits she may often disagree with her former classmate when it comes to policy, but she doesn't doubt his sincerity—or his work ethic. "He wasn't afraid to get his hands dirty; growing up on the farm, he learned to work long and hard, like all farm kids," she said. She also credits Forest City for offering an atmosphere where people could hold differing viewpoints and discuss them without animosity.

"One of the beauties of growing up in a small town like we did is that we had a good 'give-and-take' sort of environment. And, of course, the classroom skills of some exceptional teachers.

"When I think about Lura Sewick and Mr. Smith, I believe that they had a way of expecting you to discuss what you had learned," she said. "And to use what you had learned. It seemed like they really cared about their students."[21]

That viewpoint was echoed by Sally (Prickett) Brown, who also grew up in Forest City but graduated from Iowa State University and went on to an illustrious career in veterinary medicine. She has served on two state boards, appointed by governors Robert Ray and Terry Branstad, and in 2007 became director of the Lloyd Veterinary Medical Center teaching hospital at Iowa State. She also has fond memories of time spent with Sewick, who rented an apartment from her grandparents, Norm and Maude Thurston, for nearly four decades.

"It was a lovely home, and Lura lived in an upstairs bedroom," said Sally in 2014. "It was small, very small. But that was her choice, for all those years. She never had a driver's license, but the house was only a block from the school and a block or so from downtown so she could walk to work and to town.

"She wore purple almost every day; that was the color she liked best. She also played canasta several times a week with two other ladies, and they often needed a fourth, so I would play with them, although I was only in junior high. And let me tell you—those games were tough. No quarter was asked or given."[22]

Sewick did not give any quarter in school, either. She lived by a strict set of rules and enforced them in the classroom at all times. Discipline was as high a priority with her as was the subject matter of the day. Sally recalls a time when Sewick used drastic measures to "educate" a student who had a reputation for being disruptive. He was continually disregarding Sewick's instructions to stop talking during class time. One day when he persisted, she marched up the aisle to where he was seated and slapped him across the face so hard that the chair tipped over backward.

"He was tangled up in the chair, trying to get back to his feet," said Sally. "She turned and calmly walked back to her desk, sat down, and continued the lesson. The boy never acted up again, and I heard he got an A in the class. I don't know what ever became of him, but I know he graduated with us.

"It was a moment I will never forget," said Sally. "Something like that would never happen today, but it worked back then. Lura Sewick was one of the old-fashioned teachers. I don't think female teachers could even marry back then. It was her profession, her life, her passion—she was totally committed. She was very intense, and there was no capitulation when it came to teaching."[23]

Near the end of her career in Forest City, the Thurstons passed away, their house was sold, and Sewick took a room in the Mansion Museum. After retirement, she moved to her hometown of Burt, a town of about five hundred residents located forty miles west of Forest City. When friends gathered to celebrate her ninetieth birthday, among those who showed up was the governor of Iowa.

She received many awards during her forty-five-year teaching career—thirty-seven of them spent at Forest City Junior High—and in 1970 she was the only teacher in the entire state to be given the Freedoms Foundation Award by the Freedoms Foundation at Valley Forge, Pennsylvania.

Lura Sewick died in 2000 at age ninety-five, and her obituary stated that she "taught the three Rs—Rights, Respect and Responsibility—to over 5,000 students." Her legacy has lived on through the thousands of students she inspired during her forty-five years in education and in the accomplishments of her most famous pupil, Terry Branstad.

While Lura Sewick had the most profound early impact on Branstad's career, it's safe to say that it was a politician from Arizona who really changed the course of his journey and helped guide his path to the state capital in Des Moines.

Barry Goldwater's book, *The Conscience of a Conservative*, had a strong influence on many citizens all across America when it was first published in 1960. After a successful career in business in Phoenix, Goldwater ran for the United States Senate in 1952 and won the seat, beginning his first six-year term in 1953. He brought with him what some consider the most conservative view of politics in American history. He was also an admirer of Herbert Hoover, the native Iowan who was president from 1928 to 1932.

Goldwater earned the Republican nomination for the presidency in 1964, defeating New York Governor Nelson Rockefeller in a bitter, hard-fought primary battle. Against the incumbent president, Lyndon B. Johnson, he ran a campaign that centered on states' rights and fighting the spread of communism around the globe.

Goldwater won five southern states but lost everywhere else except in his native Arizona. His landslide defeat opened the door for President Johnson's Great Society program and also brought about a new and reenergized Republican Party, from which emerged a dynamic leader who had strong Iowa ties—Ronald Wilson Reagan.

Branstad's mother was a Democrat, so that was the political landscape he was most familiar with at home. She even did some work for Herschel Loveless, the Democratic governor of Iowa from 1957 to 1961. But Branstad's own political views changed when he read Goldwater's book in his junior year in high school.

"My uncle Carl, my dad's older brother, is the one who suggested I read it, in about my junior year," said Terry. "I became convinced right then that I was a fiscal conservative."[24]

Goldwater's key point was stated thusly: "Throughout history, government has proved to be the chief instrument for thwarting man's liberty. Government represents power in the hands of some men to control and regulate the lives of other men. And power, as Lord Acton said, corrupts men. 'Absolute power,' he said, 'corrupts absolutely.'"[25]

Further, he said: "I have little interest in streamlining government or in making it more efficient, for I mean to reduce its size. I do not undertake to promote welfare, for I propose to extend freedom. My aim is not to pass laws but to repeal them. It is not to inaugurate new programs but to cancel old ones that do violence to the Constitution, or that have failed in their purpose, or that impose on the people an unwarranted financial burden."[26]

Goldwater abhorred the unfettered expansion of the federal government and was determined to rein in the beast. He said it "has moved into every field in which it believes its services are needed . . . The result is a Leviathan, a vast national authority out of touch with people, and out of their control. This monopoly of power is bounded only by the will of those who sit in high places.[27]

"Our tendency to concentrate power in the hands of a few men deeply concerns me," he wrote. "We can be conquered by bombs or by subversion; but we can also be conquered by neglect—by ignoring the Constitution and disregarding the principles of limited government."[28]

He attacked the concept of runaway hand-out programs by writing that among the "great evils of Welfarism is that it transforms the individual from a dignified, industrious, self-reliant spiritual being into a dependent animal creature without his knowing it. There is no avoiding this damage to character under the welfare state."[29]

In a chapter entitled "The Perils of Power," the former senator explains what the nation's founders had in mind when they wrote the Constitution, and then asked the question: "How did our national government grow from a servant with sharply limited powers into a master with virtually unlimited powers?"[30]

It's a question that has lingered since the Goldwater era, through the leadership of both Republican and Democratic presidents and Congresses, and has worked its way down into state governments all across the land. It was a question that Terry Branstad would wrestle with during his political journey.

In the early 1980s, Goldwater looked back on the impact of his thin booklet. It was, he said, "the college student underground book of the times. It was virtually ignored by the media, most college professors and other liberals, who had long held a monopoly on the information flowing to the American people. That first printing was ten thousand copies at three dollars each. Eventually, more than four million hardcover and paperback copies were sold . . . it became a rallying cry of the right against Franklin D. Roosevelt and the liberal agenda."[31]

In his introduction to the 1990 reprinting of the book by Regnery Press, Patrick J. Buchanan described the plight of the conservative party during the 1950s, which saw the rise of Soviet imperialism around the globe, most noticeably in Cuba, just off the southern tip of Florida, and by the success of Sputnik.

"With its publication, Barry Goldwater became our champion; as his campaign (for the presidency) would become the great cause of our youth. Though 1964 would end with media mockery of The

Party That Lost Its Head, no winter would abate that spring's increase. The young conservatives, bonded and blooded [*sic*] in the lost cause of '64, would one day change the world."[32]

"We had a debate in Forest City High School on presidential candidates, and I took a group of students to see Barry Goldwater in 1964 when he came to the Mason City Airport," said Branstad. "It was quite a day . . . the same day that the old canning factory in Forest City burned to the ground. Winnebago Industries had purchased the building after the canning factory closed and was building campers, not RVs, there at the time. Luckily, no one was hurt."[33]

Branstad also fondly recalls hearing Ronald Reagan give a powerful speech in 1964 entitled "A Time for Choosing," on behalf of Goldwater. It was still two years before Reagan made his first run for governor of California (Reagan served two terms, from January 1967 through January 1975). The rousing speech catapulted Reagan onto the national political scene and left a lasting impression on the future governor of Iowa.

"Reagan was so smooth in his delivery, while Goldwater was very blunt," said Branstad. "It was quite a contrast in style."[34]

In 1965, Branstad was still influenced enough by his environment at home to join the Young Democrats, but "didn't feel very welcome," and soon they parted company. In 1966, during his sophomore year at the University of Iowa, Branstad heard young state representative Chuck Grassley give a speech for the College Republicans at the University of Iowa, and "then I got real active" in the GOP side of politics, said the future governor.

"I would say it was the concept of fiscal responsibility that attracted me strongly, and that is the main reason I became a Republican."[35]

After his presidential bid debacle, Goldwater returned to the Senate for two more six-year terms. He died in 1998 at the age of eighty-nine, but his legacy lives on, even if substantially diminished. He was an ultraconservative on fiscal issues but not social issues. He had found a multitude of converts to his vision of conservative government, including a young man in Leland, Iowa, who was destined to become the longest serving governor in history. Among those not surprised by Branstad's political success is Sally Prickett.

"My grandfather was a district court judge, and my father, Rodger, was an attorney. Terry's mother, Rita, was in a bridge club with my mother. Our parents knew each other before Terry and I knew each other," said Sally in 2014.

"My first real recollection of Terry was in junior high, when the Leland kids came to Forest City for school. He was a grade ahead of me, but I remember one day in particular, when several of us were in the hallway. We were talking about what we were going to be in life—and Terry said he was going to be the governor.

"Some of the kids laughed, but not me. I said I wanted to be a veterinarian, and there weren't any female vets at that time, so both ideas seemed ludicrous." However, she became one of the first female veterinary students to graduate from Iowa State, which was the first college in America to have a school of veterinary medicine.

"We had a bond in that regard; we were both a little different," she recalled.[36]

Sally met Anthony Prickett, a native of Scotland, in the veterinarian teaching hospital, and they were married in 1975 in Forest City. Together, they embarked upon a long and highly successful career in the field of veterinary medicine, operating an office in Cumming and eventually retiring to Glenwood.

Tony passed away in October 2013, but Governor Branstad still greatly admires their work and the time he spent with them. The feeling is mutual.

"I am extremely lucky to have the family I had and the education I received from grade school forward," said Sally. "Many persons have helped along the way. Those in the Forest City school system and associated communities—including Leland, Fertile, etc.—at that time were given an opportunity to succeed in life if they so chose.

"I consider myself a lifelong learner and relish learning something new whenever possible. An open mind is a powerful tool. I also am lucky to call Terry Branstad a friend. There is no doubt in my mind that he has helped more people in the state of Iowa than anyone else heretofore, or probably ever will."[37]

With high school behind him, Terry Branstad was ready to navigate deeper waters and to test his newfound commitment to conservative politics on a much larger scale. The caption accompanying his photo in the Forest City yearbook his senior year reads: "He admits there are two sides to every question—his and the wrong one."

In the fall of 1965, he was off to the University of Iowa to test that axiom and to begin shaping his future.

CHAPTER THREE

College, Military, and Chris

Terry Branstad and Cynthia Charlson were the only two members of the Forest City class that went to the University of Iowa that fall. Branstad worked at the Dean L. Witcher Construction Company in the Twin Cities after his first year at the University of Iowa, earning $4.15 an hour. He carried his farm work ethic with him to Iowa City, finding part-time employment the first two years in Hillcrest, a men's dorm. The third year, he worked in Burge Hall, a women's dorm, to augment his income. He also secured a National Defense Student Loan, "and it wasn't fully paid off until I became governor," he said in 2014.[38]

It was during registration at Iowa that he first met the mysterious Mr. Chester P. Dingleberry, who would be with him until his final year at college. At the start of his second semester his freshman year, Branstad and a friend faced long lines of students in the Fieldhouse, waiting to register for classes. The Fieldhouse was a vast, antiquated building where athletic contests were held, as well as physical education classes, ROTC drills, and intramural events. But Branstad and his friend, David Dallman of Britt, were thwarted in their efforts to register because they did not have the signature of a counselor on their class schedule preparation sheet. Frustrated and afraid of losing the chance to get the classes they needed, the two freshmen decided to invent "Mr. Dingleberry." They signed his name on their forms, and the people at the registration table nodded and passed them through.

"Mr. Dingleberry was our adviser all four years," said the governor with a smile in 2014. "He did a nice job advising us, as everything worked out fine."[39]

Branstad's primary field of study was political science, but he added a second major in sociology. He enjoyed the energy and excitement of campus life in Iowa City, and the affection he had harbored as a youth for Hawkeye sports continued. He attended athletic events and played on the freshman baseball team, and fondly remembers smacking a grand slam home run in one practice game. But perhaps the story that he likes to tell the most from his college days has to do with a quality that he considers among his most important assets—sincerity.

"You know, the University of Iowa is known as a rather liberal institution in many ways," he said with a smile. "I was in rhetoric class as a freshman and had just given a speech. When I was finished, one of the students said, 'I don't agree with hardly anything you said, but I don't doubt your sincerity in saying it.'"[40]

It is the essential quality that would come shining through over the next forty-some years as he carved out one of the most remarkable careers in political history, in any state. Many people may have disagreed with what Terry Branstad believed and said, but not many have disputed his sincerity or convictions.

Few persons have seen Branstad's career evolve from a better "up front" seat than Lyle Simpson, a longtime Branstad adviser and senior partner in a prestigious Des Moines law firm that bears his name. He concurs with the viewpoint of that anonymous student in rhetoric class so long ago.

"There's no question that the governor's sincerity and honesty have been a large part of what makes him so successful," said Simpson while sitting in his law firm in the Equitable Building in 2014. "Terry Branstad is a very honest, sincere person, and anyone who has been around him for any length of time knows that, and gets it. They might not agree with his positions, but they know he is sincere in his convictions."[41]

Upon graduation from Iowa, Branstad was drafted into the army. He entered the service on September 17, 1969, and was sent to basic training at Fort Polk, Louisiana. More than four decades later, two memories stand out clearly in his mind: "They had pictures posted of the various snakes in the area to be aware of," he said in 2014. "Water moccasins, cottonmouths, coral snakes, even rattlesnakes. And then there were the night drills, when you had to do the low crawl and they were shooting a machine gun with tracer bullets over your head . . . that's when you got really scared."[42]

Upon arrival at the reception station at Fort Polk, the new soldiers took an aptitude test and at the end of their eight weeks of basic training received their orders. Brandstad had taken twelve hours of criminology classes in college, so that may have led to him being assigned to the military police. Branstad was sent to Fort Gordon, Georgia, for eight weeks of schooling, and then was assigned to duty at Fort Bragg, North Carolina, one of the top military bases in the Western Hemisphere. It was founded in 1918 and today covers over 250 square miles. Named for a Confederate general in the Civil War, the base is currently the home to the US Army airborne forces and Special Forces and also served as the US Army Forces Command and US Army Reserves Command. In 1961, the camp became a center for training of counterinsurgency forces in Southeast Asia. It is estimated that over two hundred thousand service personnel underwent their basic combat training at the camp in the period between 1966 and 1970.

"I had relatives who served in World War II, and I wanted to make the most of it and use it as a learning experience," Branstad recalled in 2014. "So I was proud to serve in the army military police. I spent nearly two years in the military police; it was a great experience. I was selected as the provost marshal's driver and served in that role for over a year."[43]

The provost marshal was Colonel Hervey Keator, and despite the difference in age and rank, the two struck up a cordial relationship. Not only did Terry take the colonel's young daughters to Roller Derby, but Keator, obviously aware of Branstad's political ambitions, once told him, "When you get to be a congressman, I want to be your chief of staff."[44]

Branstad drove the colonel to meetings and was at Fort Bragg when actress Jane Fonda, who was sparking national controversy with her protesting of the Vietnam War and her alleged sympathy for the Vietcong, announced she was going to stage a protest on the base. Terry put together nineteen pages of documents on why Fonda shouldn't be allowed to do so, and the military rejected her request to visit. She came anyway and was arrested, but he personally did not make the arrest.

During his time at Fort Bragg, he was named "Soldier of the Quarter" and moved up in rank from E1 to E5 rather quickly. In a practice fairly common at the time, his service was cut short by a couple of months when he was given an early release at the end of July 1971 to go back to college.

"I was accepted for law school at both Iowa and Drake," he said. "Drake was more expensive, but with the GI Bill, I was able to afford it. The key attraction was that Drake was in the capital city, and with my interest in government it was just too big an opportunity to pass up."[45]

He made a smooth transition from soldier to law student, but once back in Iowa, a titanic change in his life was looming on the horizon. He developed a friendship with a fellow law student named John Maxwell, who had grown up in Des Moines and was dating a local girl who had a friend they thought Branstad might like. Her name was Christine Johnson, and Branstad decided to give her a call. The initial effort didn't work out well, but not because of anything that either Terry or Chris did. In fact, Chris never even got on the phone.

Christine Johnson Branstad is the oldest of five children of Richard and Clara Johnson, who met on a blind date in 1949. Richard Johnson was born and raised in tiny Duncombe, just east of Fort Dodge, while Clara was from Clare, a few miles northwest of Fort Dodge. Johnson moved to Los Angeles after working at an air force base in Utah during World War II, but came back to Iowa because "things were getting a little tough" in Los Angeles. He found employment as a surveyor for Webster County.[46]

They were married in 1951 and lived in Fort Dodge for several years, where Richard began working for Electrical Engineering and Equipment (known as Three E), and Clare worked in a local bank. When Three E closed the Fort Dodge plant, it offered Richard Johnson a job in the Des Moines operation, and the family moved south in 1954. Richard wound up a forty-year career with the company in 1990, retiring after serving as manager of the industrial sales department.

Their two oldest children, Chris and Mary, were born in Fort Dodge, while the next three—Kevin, Karen, and David—were born in Des Moines.

"I grew up in a south side, Democratic household. We didn't know any Republicans," said Chris Branstad. She attended St. Joseph's Academy, an all-girls school just down the street from Terrace Hill. "I walked past this place almost every day on my way to school and never even really looked at it," she said while sitting in the Terrace Hill mansion on February 5, 2014. St. Joseph's Academy was formed in 1885 and merged in 1972 with Dowling High School, which was established as a boys' school in 1918.[47]

Chris Branstad graduated from St. Joseph's in 1970 and attended the University of Iowa for one year. "But I wasn't too committed to studies at that point," she said, "and came home to take a job." She was working at Household Finance and living with her parents when the future governor of Iowa called her that fall evening in 1971, prepared to ask for a date.

"He called me at dinnertime, which was sacred at our house," she said with a wry smile. "You sat down at dinner, you ate everything on your plate, and you sure didn't talk to anyone on the phone. My dad answered the phone when Terry called and said, 'She doesn't take calls at dinnertime.' I was so mad at my dad—I hadn't had a date for three months, and I didn't know if he would call again."[48]

Richard Johnson chuckled when reminded of the story in the fall of 2014. "Well, we just didn't take calls at dinnertime," he said. "He was welcome to call back after dinner."[49]

Terry didn't call back that night, or the following night, because he drove to Iowa City to hear a speech by US Senator John Tower of Texas. But persistence is a Branstad trait, and Terry Branstad has exhibited plenty of it through the decades. He called back two days later and asked Chris to go to Drake homecoming festivities with him that weekend. She accepted, and the date worked out rather well, to say the least.

"We went to the homecoming football game, then to dinner, and then to a Helen Reddy concert," she said. "When he took me home, I asked him if he would like to come to Mass with me the next morning, and he said he would." She paused. "We were engaged after one month."[50]

Terry Branstad had grown up in a household with a Lutheran father and a Jewish mother. He had no Catholic background whatsoever, but within two days of meeting her, he told Chris he was going to become a Catholic. He was serious about that commitment, and very serious about building a lasting relationship with her. That Christmas, he gave her a large box. She opened the box to find another gift-wrapped box, then another. She quickly opened five boxes, and in the last one found an engagement ring.

They were married on June 17, 1972, at Christ the King Church in Des Moines. Chris Johnson had no idea what type of changes were in store for her when she agreed to become Mrs. Terry Branstad. They rented a farmhouse north of Leland, and Chris quickly adopted the Branstad family work ethic lifestyle. They were raising pigs on the farm, and Terry would head south to Des Moines three days a week for classes at Drake, a drive of nearly two hours one way, then return home to do the chores and study. Chris began working at Winnebago Industries in Forest City and tending to the farm work as much as possible.

"She was a city girl out there helping clean the barns," said Branstad, recalling the memories while sitting in the governor's office at the state capitol. "We also had some Saint Bernard puppies. I wish we had some photos of them from those days."[51]

"When we started dating, he was in his first year of law school," said Chris Branstad. "But he was running for state legislature before we were even married."[52]

Terry Branstad's desire to enter state politics had been building for years, ever since its humble origins back in eighth grade in Forest City when he boldly declared to a teacher and classmates that he would someday be governor. After fulfilling his military obligation and opting for Drake Law School over Iowa, he found himself immersed in a political environment that fueled his vision. Everywhere he turned in Des Moines, politics was a hot topic—on the radio, in the *Des Moines Register*, and around campus.

Then, in the fall of 1972, the Iowa Supreme Court struck down the legislative reapportionment plan and announced its own plan. That decision moved back the filing deadline for the primary. When word came that there was no incumbent in the new district, which included Winnebago County, Branstad suddenly saw a window of opportunity, and he seized it. He decided to run for state legislature in House District Eight, which represented Forest City, Leland, and Lake Mills, as well as the northern part of Kossuth County and eleven of the twelve townships in Emmet County. The area had a strong conservative tradition, and Terry Branstad was ready to make his move.

Ironically, the Democratic Party of Iowa played a key role in the emergence of its greatest adversary. While it was customary for the legislature to reapportion districts every decade, in 1971 the Democrats decided to challenge the decision. The League of Women Voters joined in, and the case went all the way to the Iowa Supreme Court, which threw it out. It was that lawsuit that ended up creating District 8, which included all of Winnebago County and parts of Hancock County, an area where Terry Branstad felt very much at home.

"It was their lawsuit that ended up creating District Eight," he said in 2014. "And that was when I decided to run." However, the person he had to convince to support him wasn't his wife, Chris—it was his own mother. Rita Branstad had worked on the campaign for Governor Herschel Loveless years earlier and was a staunch Democrat. But she had other worries besides her son's political persuasion.

"My mother was concerned that I wouldn't finish law school, and I told her not to worry—that I would. My dad wasn't that optimistic, either," Branstad recalled.[53] But he managed to convince them both that he could actively campaign and handle law school and the farm at the same time. Not only did he persuade his mother that he could do it, he talked her into helping him campaign, which meant she also had to become a Republican.

Rita Branstad also had one other piece of advice for her son. "Mom said you're never going to get elected with a moustache," he recalled with a chuckle. "She wanted me to get rid of it, but Chris said not to cut it off. So . . ." Through the years, the moustache has become a subject of continual conversation around the state. It has been made fun of by some and embraced by others, but it has never left his face. Even into the campaign of 2014, his facial etching on political mailings emphasized the moustache.

"In April of 1972, we went to a women's event in Estherville," he recalled. "I didn't know anyone there at all. But Rollie Edelen, the representative from the Estherville–Spirit Lake area, sat down with me and told me the key people to approach for assistance in the eleven townships of Emmet County."[54]

So there he was, taking ten hours of classes at Drake, driving to Des Moines three times a week, raising pigs and doing farm chores with Chris (who was also working full time), and running as a candidate for the state legislature at night. His opponent was Elmer Leibrand, the mayor of Buffalo Center, and Branstad garnered 59 percent of the vote en route to victory. The total tally was 7,368 votes for Branstad and 5,130 for Leibrand.

In January 1973, at age twenty-six and walking into the state capitol for the first time as a member of the state legislature, he was on his way to becoming an Iowa political icon. But he also had to earn a living. Branstad graduated from law school in August 1974 and shortly after became co-owner of a law firm in Lake Mills, just ten miles northeast of Leland. He and Richard Schwarm were partners in the firm until he was elected governor in 1982.

Schwarm was the son of a Methodist minister and spent his early years in South Dakota. The family moved to Sioux City, Iowa, when he was in eighth grade, where he graduated from high school and then earned his bachelor's degree from Morningside College, located in Sioux City. He met Terry Branstad at a Young Republicans meeting when he was a sophomore at Morningside, and they formed a friendship. He earned his law degree at Drake, where he and Branstad were classmates and friends.

Terry Branstad had planned to buy into a Lake Mills law firm because the senior partner, Dean Brackey, was leaving to run a bank. Brackey's partner was Richard Ramsey, who was diagnosed with cancer and died rather suddenly. Branstad then negotiated with Roger Brown, the attorney for Ramsey's estate, to buy the firm from Ramsey's widow.

"It was a two-partner firm, and I was kidding Terry a bit about that, asking him how he was going to keep up with the work load," said Schwarm in 2014. "Terry said that it was a great deal and he'd like to sell me half. I thought about it for thirty hours or so and decided that's what I wanted to do. We had known each other for several years through politics and law school, and I felt we would work well together."[55]

It was a very hectic time. Branstad bought the law practice in May, sold half to Schwarm, passed the bar that same month (but still had several hours left to go at Drake), and graduated in August. Terry and Chris purchased an acreage and lived near Lake Mills long enough that many people actually thought he was born, raised, and attended high school there. Even today, a sign on the outskirts of Lake Mills declares that it is the home of Governor Branstad, and the city's website lists him among its notable citizens.

Branstad ran unopposed in the 1974 primary and romped to a huge victory in the general election that year, riding on his conservative philosophy. He attracted 6,699 votes as compared to 3,046 for his Democratic opponent, Jean Haugland. He was unopposed again in the 1976 primary and had another easy time in the general election, more than doubling the vote of his foe, Franklin Banwart, to win a third term. The final margin was 8,553 for Branstad and just 3,600 for Banwart.

Chris eventually left her job at Winnebago and began working for her husband as a clerk in the legislature, and it wasn't smooth sailing all the time. "We were the only couple (in the legislature) that yelled at each other—and the only couple that cried together," she recalled. "But we made it work."[56]

Basically shy by nature, Chris recoiled from the thought of being continually in the public eye, and giving any sort of speech was almost beyond her imagination. "Terry loves it, but I'm missing that particular gene," she said in 2014. However, she got talked into stumping for her husband a few times.

"She went out and campaigned for me in 1978, in the primary race for lieutenant governor," said Terry Branstad. "It was a debate in Hampton; the House was in session, and I needed to be there. I sent my twenty-five-year-old wife, who had no interest in politics, out there to take my place. Afterward, she said she'd never do that again. But we carried the county, so she must have done pretty well.

"You have to make it fun. I love to get to know people and places and history. All of that is the key to me."[57]

At the very outset, Chris Branstad made the adjustment to life in the hectic world of politics. "I was a very naive person. I just thought, 'This is what my husband wants, and I'm here to support him,'" she said in 2014, reflecting back on his long political career. "To this day I can't get into campaigning, but I love being here in Terrace Hill. I have lived here now longer than anyplace else."[58]

Terry Branstad earned a reputation in northern Iowa as a hard-working and dedicated legislator and attorney. As with any person starting out in an occupation, there were a few rough spots along the way. One of his involved a perpetual troublemaker from the Forest City area who had been arrested yet again, but had no money for an attorney. Branstad was appointed by the court to be his defense attorney. Eager to do a good job, Branstad did his homework and then asked for a meeting with the prosecutor in order to plea-bargain his client's case. They agreed to meet at the courthouse with the defendant in the room. After conferring, Branstad asked the prosecutor for a private talk outside the room. He told his client to stay put while they talked. Since the prisoner was on the second floor of the courthouse and a police guard was stationed outside the room, there seemed to be no risk in leaving him alone.

After their hallway meeting, Branstad walked back into the room—and immediately came back out. "Where's my client?" he asked the startled officer. "He's not in there!"

They discovered that the prisoner had opened the window, climbed out, and leaped from the second floor into the grass and run off. He was apprehended several hours later in Mason City. It is a story that has survived in the Forest City area for over three decades, said Dan Davis, police chief in 2014.[59]

Working long, tough hours and driving from Lake Mills to Des Moines for legislative sessions paid off for Branstad. After six years in the state legislature, the Leland native had earned a reputation for his hard work, honesty, and considerable organizational skills.

The 1978 election created a vacuum in the position of lieutenant governor in the state. Republican Arthur Neu was retiring from politics to pursue a private law practice in his hometown of Carroll. After graduating with a law degree from Northwestern University in Evanston, Illinois, Neu became mayor of Carroll, then won a seat in the Iowa State Senate. In 1972, he ran for lieutenant governor and won, replacing Roger Jepsen.

After two terms as Robert Ray's lieutenant governor, Neu opted to return to full-time private practice back home. Branstad, nearing the end of his third term in the Iowa House, decided it was time to move up the political ladder. He declared he would run for the open spot and, despite little encouragement from the Ray faction, jumped into the race full scale. He faced two opponents for lieutenant governor in the primary: fellow Republicans Bill Hansen and Brice Oakley, both of them state legislators Branstad knew well, also threw their hats in the ring for the state's second-highest position.

Hansen, an insurance executive and real estate agent, was raised in Hancock County and was a graduate of Cedar Falls High School and Dana College in Blair, Nebraska. He served two terms in the Iowa State House and two terms in the Iowa State Senate, where he held the position of assistant minority leader from 1975 to 1978.

Oakley was born in Washington, Iowa, and graduated from Roosevelt High School in Des Moines. He received his bachelor's degree in public administration, followed by a law degree, both from the University of Iowa. Oakley was a state representative from Clinton in District 78 and later became legal counsel on Governor Ray's staff.

Two key people in Branstad's decision to run for lieutenant governor were Mike Forest and Lyle Simpson. The latter has a long involvement with Branstad, both as a consultant and a friend. Coming from humble origins in Des Moines—his father ran a small grocery store—he used his engaging personality and sharp intellect to become president of the student body at Drake in 1960, whereheand graduated from Drake law school. He joined the Iowa National Guard while still a senior in high school and rose to the rank of second lieutenant. He entered law practice in 1964 and is president of the Simpson, Jensen, Abels, Fischer and Bouslog law firm. He has a long history with the governor, serving as his legal counsel and on the inaugural committee of 1982, 1986, 1990, 1994, and 2010. He was also a member of the Governor's Council Cabinet from 1983 through 1999.

"Mike Forest was the guy who introduced me to Terry," said Simpson in 2014. "Mike is an attorney and was a lobbyist who had worked with Terry and was impressed by him. When Terry decided to run for governor, he knew he would need advice from several areas. In January of 1978, Terry called me over to the state house to talk about running for lieutenant governor and to see if I would help. Mike had told me Terry might call, so I had done some research on him. We went to the law library. I had done enough research on him to know that he was highly regarded in his district and respected on both sides of the aisle. He had integrity beyond reproach. I hesitated because he's far more conservative than me on social issues, but we agreed on most everything else."[60]

Simpson agreed to serve as an adviser, as he had for Lieutenant Governor Roger Jepsen several years earlier, and on March 1, 1978, Simpson hosted a Branstad fundraiser at his home. He and his wife at the time lived in a six-thousand-square-foot house with nineteen rooms, on the highest point in Des Moines. He lived there for thirty years and sold it in 2004. A huge crowd of around 550 people showed up for the party.

"It was snowing, and people had to park a mile away and walk to the house," said Simpson. "It started at five thirty, but Terry arrived almost two hours later, because that was the night the legislature passed the bottle bill, which he had cosponsored. He wasn't going to leave until it was passed. When I saw the size of the turnout, and how people had to walk through snow to get there, that told me he was electable."

Simpson saw even more than the lieutenant governor's position in Branstad's future. "That night, Terry's mother, Rita, and

I walked into the family room and looked out over the city. We could see Terrace Hill from there," recalled Simpson. "I pointed to it and said to his mother, 'We're going to get your son there.' She was a bit startled."[61]

But while some Republicans regarded Branstad as a good choice for the position of lieutenant governor, not everyone in the party was of that mind-set. In fact, Governor Ray actually supported Oakley. Several members of the Ray staff made less than flattering comments about Branstad and often looked upon him as a young upstart without a great deal of depth.

"Frankly, some of those people viewed Terry as a lightweight," said Doug Gross in 2014. A graduate of Iowa Wesleyan College in Mount Pleasant who earned his law degree from Drake in 1985, Gross was speaking from the perspective of having worked closely with both camps. He was an administrative assistant to Ray during his last term as governor and then served as Branstad's chief of staff from 1984 to 1989.

"The fact is, people were always underestimating Terry Branstad. He is a master politician, the best I have ever seen. And he never holds a grudge. When he became governor, he kept most of Ray's staff, because he knew that they were good at what they did and could make him a better governor. He is very pragmatic in that regard."

And, said Gross, "he never keeps an enemy."[62]

Simpson admitted that it would be a tough road: "My initial reaction was we may not get him there the first time but we will the second time." Both Hansen and Oakley had stronger name recognition at the time.[63]

The new campaign received an unexpected boost when a young man who was in his third year of studies at the University of Northern Iowa became involved. Randy Smith had a background similar to Terry Branstad's, having grown up in Whiting, a small town thirty miles from Sioux City. He got his first real taste of politics in 1977 as a summer intern working in the Washington, DC, office of Chuck Grassley, who was a United States congressman at the time (he became a US senator in 1981). There, Smith roomed with John

Maxwell, who was an administrative assistant in Grassley's office and who had introduced Terry and Chris.

"When I returned to school, John called and said he had a friend who was running for lieutenant governor and asked if I wanted to get involved," said Smith in 2015. "John had already talked to Terry about me."

Smith connected with Branstad, and they hit it off immediately. On March 1, 1978, Smith was appointed the campaign's organizational director. Several weeks later, at the age of twenty-two, Smith was elevated to campaign manager. After the election, Smith returned to UNI and earned a degree in accounting and has enjoyed a long and successful career, living in Houston, Texas, for the past three decades. He harbors fond memories of his short time with the Branstad campaign.

"It was an amazing experience," he said. "We'd be up and moving at dawn every day, going to coffees and meetings nonstop, until late at night. Our motto was that they (the opposition) can outspend us but they can't outwork us."

Though Smith said he had no idea that what they were building back in 1978 would end up with Branstad becoming a political icon, he is not surprised at the governor's record-breaking successes.

"I've met a lot of politicians over the years, and most were very nice people, but Terry Branstad is the most normal one of the whole bunch," said Smith. "He is just so natural and unassuming in the way he interacts with people. It was an experience that I will never forget."[64]

Nor is he likely to forget one very dramatic flight that occurred during that time. He was in a small plane with Terry and Chris Branstad, headed for a fundraiser in Sioux City. Senator Bob Dole was the featured guest for the event, which was set up by Jack Robinson. As they approached the airport, Smith, who was sitting next to the pilot, asked him when he knew the landing gear was down.

The pilot was Jack Clark of Altoona, Iowa, a veteran of World War II, and his wife, Gilda, was also on the plane, a Skymaster push-pull aircraft with two engines.

"He pointed to the instrument panel and said he'd know it was down when the three lights came on," said Smith. "Well, the lights weren't on. He said he'd give it another few seconds . . . but the lights still didn't come on. He then called the flight tower and asked if they could see the landing gear as we did a flyby. They confirmed it was not down.

"We went back up quite a ways, and then he put the plane on autopilot and pulled out the instrument book and began reading, saying he wanted to find out what was wrong. He tried a few maneuvers in the air, trying to bounce the wheels out, and flew by the tower three or four more times to see if the wheels were down."

Then things got wild. The pilot read that there was a reservoir near the instrument panel in which fluid could be poured to perhaps loosen up the landing gear. However, there was no fluid in the tiny plane. A cup was passed to see if the three men could urinate enough to pour fluid in the reservoir, but that didn't work either.

"What we didn't know until afterward was that when the wheels came up (on takeoff) they had cut one of the reservoir lines," said Smith. "No amount of fluid would have helped."

After almost two hours of flying around above the airport, the pilot took the plane down without landing gear. The plane landed in the grass, belly up, and bounced onto the runway. All five departed, quickly.

"We weren't scared while up in the air. It didn't really hit us until later, when we were on the ground," said Smith. "We had missed the fundraiser, and an hour later we were on a larger plane on our way back to Des Moines, where Terry had a debate . . . and he did great." Senator Dole gave his talk and then came to the airport to greet the Branstad group to make sure they were okay.[65]

It was the first of several narrow escapes that Branstad would experience with planes over the coming years.

On the other side of the aisle, two Democrats vied for the nomination for lieutenant governor. Minnette Doderer was born near Holland, Iowa, and graduated from Waterloo East High School. She earned a bachelor's degree from the University of Iowa and started a political career by winning a special election to the Iowa House of Representatives in 1964. Doderer went on to serve in the Iowa

Senate from 1969 to 1978, and became the first female president pro tempore of the Iowa Senate in 1975 and 1976.

William Palmer was born in Iowa City, graduated from East Des Moines High School, and eventually became president of Palmer and Associates Inc. He represented the Thirty-Second district located in Des Moines as part of the state house for two terms and then went on to the state senate.

The primary election was June 6, 1978. For the Democrats, Palmer accumulated 53,277 votes to Doderer's 50,049. Branstad easily outpaced his opponents by garnering 61,078 votes to Hansen's 47,427 and Oakley's 36,565 votes. Suddenly the brash young man from Leland was poised for a giant step forward in the Iowa political scene.

"Terry got the nomination because he was so well organized," said Simpson. "That is one of his real strengths. He just out-organized everyone else."[66] Gross and another key adviser, David Fisher, agreed, and all three said his work ethic also paid off handsomely as he traveled to all ninety-nine counties, working indefatigably to get his message, and name, in front of the voters.

During the general election, Branstad ran the same well-organized campaign throughout the state. In the November 7, 1978, general election, Branstad won handily, racking up 451,928 votes to 330,817 for Palmer.

The young man from Leland was closing in on his boyhood dream of becoming governor. Among the Iowans who were not caught off guard were Richard and Clare Johnson. ""We liked him right off the bat," said Richard. "He was a doer . . . he got things done, and he loved politics." Clare agreed: "He was always so serious and so determined to succeed. And he made a very good first impression."[67]

In January 1979, Terry Branstad became the youngest lieutenant governor in Iowa history, at age thirty-two. He had come a long way in a remarkably short period of time, but there was much more success on the road ahead.

CHAPTER FOUR

Chasing the Top Prize
(The Election of 1982)

The office of lieutenant governor is not generally a glamorous or highly important one in most states, and that was certainly the case for Iowa in the 1970s and '80s. Branstad's main job was to preside over the senate and to appoint the chairperson and members to each of the standing committees in the senate. In addition, the lieutenant governor serves as a figurehead for events that the governor is not able to attend. But the position also provided the young politician from Leland the opportunity to observe the intricacies of the office he coveted from an up close perspective, and to learn from a master politician in the person of Bob Ray.

Branstad was honored for his victory with an open house at the Helgeson Civic Center in Lake Mills and then settled into his new office at the state capitol in mid-January to begin his duties. In late November 1979, he celebrated his thirty-third birthday at the River Oaks Clubhouse in Forest City, with nearly one hundred Winnebago County supporters in attendance. The event also served as the kickoff of a new program called "Lieutenant Governor's Club," with the goal of raising funds for Branstad to travel the state for public appearances, as such expenses were not covered by state funds.

He served quietly during his first term as lieutenant governor, but was studying and learning all the time and making valuable connections. As his first term was winding down, there was speculation that Ray might not run for a fifth term as governor, and many Iowans wondered what Terry Branstad's plans were for the immediate future. On October 8, 1981, he gave an interview to the *Forest City Summit* to address that situation.

"It (is) time that I ended all the speculation going around that I might run for Congress from the sixth district, or run for governor," Branstad told the *Summit*. He said he was going to run for a second term as lieutenant governor. And then he added: "If Governor Ray decides not to run for reelection I will be interested in running for governor."[68]

Speculation about the local boy someday soon moving into Terrace Hill was rampant in the Leland–Forest City–Lake Mills area. In his popular column "Iowa Boy" in the *Des Moines Register*, Chuck Offenburger had added fuel to the fire back on November 23, 1980:

"Winnebago County residents have recognized for two years that one of their own, Terry Branstad, is just a step away from being governor of Iowa. But in the past couple of weeks, that feeling has changed around here. Now, the talk is that Branstad, the 34-year-old lieutenant governor is a half step away.

"'No, make that a quarter step,' said Hilma Singelstad, a secretary in Branstad's law firm and a lifelong resident of the community. 'People who have talked about going down to Des Moines to visit Terrace Hill, well, now they're saying we might as well wait until Terry gets in there.'

"And Dean Brackey, president of the Farmers and Merchants State Bank here (in Lake Mills), added, 'This is a lot of fun and excitement in a small town, you know? People view it as quite an honor that we could be the hometown of the governor before long.' The enthusiasm for all this goes beyond Lake Mills to Branstad's other two hometowns—Leland, located near the farm where he was reared, and Forest City, where he went to high school."[69]

In the column, Branstad confided that he had received a phone call from President Reagan: "'He called to thank me for my support over the years,' Branstad said. 'We talked for eight or ten minutes, and it was very nice.'" It was obvious that such a phone call would look good on anyone's resume.

But a major announcement by Robert Ray was about to change everything. The end of an era in Iowa politics was on the horizon as Ray was weighing his options after a record fourteen years in office. His astute governing style and engaging personality made him one of the most effective and popular politicians the state has ever seen.

Born and raised in Des Moines, Ray graduated from Drake University with a BA in business and then a law degree. He worked in the capital city, giving him a head start when he entered into politics. As governor, Ray championed civil rights, energy conservation, and government efficiencies and created numerous committees and commissions to strengthen the state in various ways. Governor Ray's humanitarian legacy remains a high point for his administration as he helped save thousands of lives by working with President Gerald Ford and the State Department to welcome refugees from war-torn Southeast Asia to the state.

During Ray's third term, the governor's term of office was changed from two to four years, and in 1976, he and his wife, Billie, became the first governor's family to live at Terrace Hill. Before Terrace Hill became the home of the sitting governor, the chief executive of the state would purchase a house in Des Moines or rent a place of residence. That practice eventually was retired, and from 1949 through 1976, the sitting governor lived at 2900 Grand Avenue, which meant the Rays only had to move six blocks to Terrace Hill.

An eighteen-thousand-square-foot second empire architecture-styled mansion, Terrace Hill was built in 1869 by businessman Benjamin Franklin Allen for $250,000. Only a few years later, the nation's economy turned sour with the farm crisis of the 1880s, and in 1884, Allen was forced to sell his elegant home to F. M. Hubbell for $55,000. Hubbell lived in the house until his death in 1930, and during a 1971 ceremony, his family bequeathed Terrace Hill to the state of Iowa. In 1972, the state of Iowa authorized the mansion for the purpose of the governor's official home, with accessibility to the general public. In 1976, after renovations to the newly designated third-floor governor's quarters, Governor Ray and his family moved in. Two years later, the historical site was opened to the public. Since then, an average of thirty thousand visitors tour the mansion annually.

Riding on his successes and popularity, Governor Ray was able to easily defeat all of his Democratic opponents in five straight elections. In his last gubernatorial election, in November 1978, Ray gained 58.3 percent of the vote for a lopsided win over his Democrat challenger, Jerry Fitzgerald, who accumulated just 40.9 percent.

By the time he was contemplating leaving office, however, the state was seeing the effects of the nationwide recession and the looming farm crisis. In August 1982, an estimated 8.3 percent of the state's work force of 1.4 million was out of work—a 1.7 percent jump from the year before. With the inclusion of seasonal labor, that number fluctuated as high as 11.4 percent unemployment in the state. The national unemployment hovered at 9.8 percent, and in September of that year it climbed to 10.1 percent. Unemployment, low agriculture prices, and high interest rates would be the center of the debate to determine the next governor in the 1982 elections.

The political landscape was also changing across Iowa and the nation. A *New York Times* article published in the fall of 1982 noted that politicians were becoming more aware of a "gender gap" (a difference in political attitude between men and women) in campaigns across the country. The year before, national polls clearly indicated women's discontent with President Ronald Reagan's economic and budget policies. There was some serious consideration across the nation, including in Iowa, that the climate was ripe for a women's candidate at high office.

In 2014, Branstad recalled how events transpired: "I was intending to run for lieutenant governor again. I had supported the governor when I could and was very quiet when I had to be. But there was speculation that Ray might not run for another term. It was less than a month to go before filing deadline when we got the word. In February, he called in the legislative leaders of the GOP and said he had decided he was not going to run. I was surprised.

"I called my wife and said, 'Here we go!'"[70]

Ray's announcement, combined with a struggling statewide economy, gave Democrats their best opportunity in years to capture the state's highest office. But it also provided Terry Branstad with the opportunity of a lifetime.

"Not unlike many successful politicians, Branstad benefitted from fortuitous timing," wrote James Strohman in a major article appearing in *CityView* in 2014. "When the popular Governor Robert Ray decided to step down in 1982, Branstad was finishing his first term as lieutenant governor and was in an ideal position to win the GOP nomination, having already established a statewide organization and a reputation as a solid and authentic conservative. Remarkably, he was able to avoid a primary challenge."[71]

Once his decision was made to run, he began building support immediately. He visited six cities across the state to make official announcements of his plan. The first stop was at the Mason City airport on March 4, and the new candidate was greeted by nearly 250 supporters. He made a long speech, outlining his plans.

"Last week, Governor Ray surprised most Iowans with his decision not to seek reelection. Since that announcement, I have received encouragement and support from a wide range of people who have asked me to run for governor.

"After thoughtful consultation with my wife, law partner, and friends, I have decided to announce my intention to seek the office of governor of Iowa. I approach this campaign with a positive attitude, great enthusiasm, and total dedication to building a better Iowa. We can build on the strong foundation of the fine record established by Governor Ray and Republican state leadership.

"We can build on the tradition of balanced budgets and living within our means.

"We can build on a history of progress with stability.

"Between now and the end of this legislative session, I intend to devote most of my time to working with Governor Ray and the legislature to pass the 1982 legislative program.

"In the near future, I intend to appoint various advisory committees to assist me in formulating my approach to the key issues confronting Iowa. I will seek out the advice of people who have the expertise, the experience, and knowledge to help me meet the challenges facing Iowa.

"Making Iowa attractive to business is the key to preserving jobs and creating new jobs. I have a consistent record of support for business. Improving our state economy and providing more jobs is my top priority.

"Iowa's educational programs are recognized for their excellence. We must maintain the quality of these programs and make more job opportunities available here in Iowa for the graduates.

"As a lifelong farm resident, I am keenly aware that Iowa's future depends on agriculture. Farmers deserve a tax system that treats them fairly. I helped eliminate the personal property tax on livestock and based real estate taxes on income productive capacity, rather than inflated market values. We have made progress in solving Iowa's soil conservation problem, but much more needs to be done.

"For the last two years in my opening remarks to the Iowa Senate, I have spoken out for stronger criminal laws. Some progress was made last year, and more is likely to pass this session. Support for law enforcement, assistance for victims of crimes, and greater public safely will continue to be one of my priorities.

"Senior citizens have expressed their concern about cuts in federal programs. In Iowa, I believe that the state must protect our elderly from cuts in essential services.

"Throughout my career, I have actively sought the opinions of all Iowans . . . Republicans, Democrats, and Independents. Throughout my term as lieutenant governor, I talked with thousands of Iowans in cafés, on their farms, in factories, in schools, and in their homes.

"During the campaign I will address the issues honestly, fairly, and compassionately. With ten years of service in state government, I am confident that as governor I can meet the test.

"We will conduct a positive campaign that appeals to the common sense and good judgment of the people of Iowa. I plan to reach out to all kinds of people from all walks of life in all parts of the state. Our six stops today are just the beginning. I will campaign in all ninety-nine counties.

"I must rely on you, the people of Iowa, to help carry our message of reassurance, hope, and progress to your friends and neighbors. We need the help of thousands of Iowans, young and old, male and female, urban, small towns, and rural. With your dedicated help we will be successful."[72]

Branstad recruited some key Ray people for his team, including business leader Jack Peester—"even though I was rural and conservative." He also assembled a small group of associates that he conferred with for advice and support. Lyle Simpson called it "a sort of kitchen cabinet"; the group consisted of Simpson, Marvin Pomerantz, Dave Fisher, and Janet Lyons.

They had all played key roles, especially Pomerantz. Born in Des Moines in 1930, he rose from very humble family origins to become one of the most influential businessmen in state history. He was an entrepreneur, real estate developer, and philanthropist of the highest rank, and today the Pomerantz Career Center on the University of Iowa campus helps develop leaders of tomorrow. One of his top employees, Dick Redman, was an expert in finance who also lent his considerable expertise to the Branstad campaign.

Simpson "was selected" to tell Branstad there were five criteria the group wanted him to meet: (1) he had to quit driving alone because he had a tendency to get sleepy behind the wheel and endanger himself; (2) he had to buy a couple of new, conservative-style suits; (3) he had to take some speech lessons to improve his delivery; (4) he had to lose some weight; and (5) Chris had to agree to participate, at least on some level.

"He was agreeable to all five," said Simpson. About the suits and weight, Simpson said, "He looked like a college kid—we were trying to mature him, make him look older."[73]

The five-point plan was adopted, and Branstad was off and running, adding his own considerable talents to the mix. According to David Fisher, an attorney/businessman who has served as one of Branstad's top advisers for nearly three decades, it was Branstad's organizational skills and solid reputation that held off any primary challengers. "One of the keys to his success is that he always raised money early, and that discouraged others from even getting in," said Fisher in 2014, sitting in his office at the Des Moines Airport.

One of Fisher's first impressions of Branstad is etched firmly in his mind almost three decades later. "Back in the eighties, I was on my way to the Des Moines YMCA about five a.m. for a running workout," said Fisher. "The streets were empty. I looked over at the car next to me and saw Terry sitting there. He was going out to campaign somewhere, at five a.m. I remember thinking, 'Wow, that guy is really dedicated.' I was impressed.

"When he decided to run for governor, he was not well known in the Des Moines business community. The lieutenant governor's job was mostly ceremonial back then. He really didn't have a lot to do, other than presiding over the senate. I heard him give a speech not long after that, and I told my wife that he was going to be our next governor. He had a knack of connecting with the people, and he was very passionate."[74]

Fisher grew up in Boone and graduated from Grinnell College and then the University of Iowa law school in 1962. He started a wholesale business called Onthank Company in Des Moines and served as its chairman and CEO for fifty-two years. He entered politics when Norman Erbe, also from Boone, asked him to be his driver while he was campaigning around the state for governor back in 1960. Erbe was governor for one term, losing the 1962 election to Democrat Harold Hughes.

During the 1982 campaign trips, Fisher traveled with Branstad twice a week and marveled at his stamina, his enthusiasm, and his ability to relate to the everyday folks he met.

"He just kept going and going; he never seemed to tire," said Fisher. "When he meets people, he remembers if had met them before and can talk to them about their kids, or whatever. He works the crowd better than anyone. Robert Ray once told me that Terry Branstad is the best campaigner he ever saw, and I agree."[75]

However, there were a few tough spots along the road. On one of the latter campaigns, Branstad, Fisher, and two others were in a small twin-engine plane headed for Harlan, a town west of Des Moines. They were poring over some details in a notebook when the plane ran into rough weather. The turbulence bounced them around so hard that Fisher's head hit the ceiling—"and I was wearing my seat belt," he said—scaring the heck out of him and everyone else. The pilot even flew down to the Missouri border trying to circumvent the storm, but wound up landing in Harlan some time later.

"It was a very frightening experience," Fisher said. "We walked through the small airport pretty shaken up. There were some women sitting at a table in the lobby playing cards, and they didn't even look up. We went to where the governor gave a speech to about five people. I told him that the headline the next day could have been that three men died trying to get five votes!"[76]

Susan Neely, now president and CEO of the American Beverage Association, has a long and impressive list of accomplishments at all levels of government. One of the architects of the nation's first Department of Homeland Security, she now runs the $140 billion nonalcoholic beverage industry headquartered in Washington, DC. A graduate of the University of Iowa with a master's degree from Drake, she served as Branstad's campaign press secretary in 1982, and vividly recalls some of the traveling experiences from that period.

"We did everything on the cheap, which meant using all volunteer pilots," said Neely in 2014. "I remember some harrowing landings on airstrips in cornfields in order to get where we had to go. The state Republican ticket did a fly-around to the six media markets right after the primary. The pilot must have hit every air pocket.

"After bumping around in the air all day, all of the state ticket except Terry was green around the gills. He has a useful ability to never seem to sweat or show outward discomfort, including never having to take off his jacket. For my own part after that flight, I had such bad vertigo that I drove home and lay on the lawn, waiting for the sky to stop spinning. Terry just went on to an evening event."[77] It was a moment eerily reminiscent of the scary flight near Sioux City back in 1978 with Randy Smith.

On another occasion, after Branstad spoke at a gathering, the staff members left to go their separate ways. It was late at night, and while driving to his home in Lake Mills, Branstad hit an icy spot in the road, and the car slid off of Interstate 35 south of Clear Lake and struck a bridge pillar. Fortunately he was unharmed.

Fisher also recalled that it was important to update Branstad's apparel. He was fond of wearing polyester suits, and the team wanted him to have a more businesslike appearance, so they took him to Reichardt's, a popular clothing store in Des Moines, and bought him some more professional-looking attire.

"Linda Shawver was his first fundraiser, and she was a very sharp lady," said Fisher. "When he showed up in Clinton in one of the polyester suits, she let him have it. She said, 'Governor, if I ever see you in one of those suits again, I'll quit.'" Fisher said that another of Branstad's winning qualities is the ability to take critiques and digest them without any trace of rancor. He just accepts the advice and moves on.[78]

For the Democrats, a three-way race emerged in their primary for the governor's spot in 1982. Edward "Ed" Campbell, Jerome "Jerry" Fitzgerald, and Roxanne Conlin all threw their hats in the ring to decide who would win the right to face Branstad in the general election.

Campbell, a real estate businessman, had been a stalwart in the Democratic Party for decades. In 1965, he became an aide to Governor Harold Hughes and followed him to Washington after Hughes became a senator. In 1974, Campbell ran John Culver's campaign for the US Senate. Afterward, Campbell was chairman of the Iowa Democratic Party from 1977 to 1982.

Fitzgerald was a civil engineer and the 1978 Democratic nominee who lost by almost eighteen points to incumbent Governor Robert Ray. According to a UPI article, he said that Ray's decision not to seek reelection "'enhanced' his decision to run." He estimated at the time of his entry in the race that he would need to raise between $100,000 and $150,000 for his campaign.

Conlin was a former US attorney, and when asked by an Iowa City West High School student what kind of Democrat she was—"Are you a Hubert Humphrey liberal, a Jimmy Carter centrist, or a Shirley Chisholm populist/radical?"—she had a ready response.

"A little bit of background might be helpful," Conlin said. "I was born in South Dakota, which is where Hubert Humphrey was born. Jimmy Carter appointed me the United States attorney for the southern district of Iowa, and in 1972, I was statewide coordinator for Shirley Chisholm's (presidential) campaign."[79]

A self-described "little girl from the wrong side of the tracks," Conlin was hired for her first job at age fourteen. The ambitious young woman was accepted to Drake University at the age of sixteen without completing high school and earned her bachelor's degree in three years. She combined her senior year in college with her first year of law school and graduated with a law degree at the age of twenty-one. She was later appointed assistant Iowa attorney general and became the US attorney for the southern district of Iowa in 1977. She helped found the National Women's Political Caucus and had the support of feminist groups in her effort to succeed Robert Ray.

While conventional wisdom at the time was that Fitzgerald had the best chance for a victory in the general election, many in the party thought they had a shot at electing the first woman governor, and the excitement of such an historic moment prevailed. Polling data found most Iowans said it would not make any difference to them if a woman became governor, but in the same survey most said they thought it would make a difference to their neighbors.

In May 1982, the *Des Moines Register's* Iowa poll showed Conlin with a wide lead, being preferred by 44 percent of the likely Democratic voters. Fitzgerald followed with 24 percent, while 15 percent favored Campbell and 17 percent were undecided. The Iowa poll had Branstad trailing Conlin by seven percentage points if she became the Democratic nominee.

During the primary campaign, Conlin promised to voluntarily release her taxes, but she said she could not deliver them before the primary election because she and her husband, James, a Des Moines real estate broker, had a complex tax return and needed additional preparation time before filing. They petitioned for and received an extension on the deadline for their filing.

On June 6, 1982, Conlin emerged as the winner of the Democratic primary by a substantial margin. She garnered 94,481 votes (48 percent) compared to 61,340 votes (31 percent) for Fitzgerald and 40,233 votes (20 percent) for Campbell. Branstad, running unopposed, collected 128,314 votes.

With high unemployment, low agriculture prices, and high interest rates, Iowans understood that the need for strong leadership was vital. Once the general election campaign was underway, stark differences in the philosophy of governing became immediately apparent. The two candidates clashed on the economy, reforming taxes, rebuilding state roads and bridges, and financing post-secondary education.

Conlin campaigned to divert the onus of funding education from property taxes to other forms of taxation. "The property tax is the most unfair tax there is, and yet we use it to finance education," she stated. To jump-start the tepid economy, Conlin wanted $300 million worth of general obligation bonds to attract new industry to the state. The money would be used to improve the state's roads and railways to make Iowa an attractive place for businesses to settle.

"It is a plan that will assist us in revitalizing our economy no matter what Washington does," she said. "Trickle-down economics doesn't work. It never has and it never will. This (bonding proposal) is trickle-up."[80]

She promised that she wouldn't raise taxes "willy-nilly" but would assess the need before making any tax changes. If increases were necessary, she proposed raising the state sales tax before any other form of taxation.

Conlin also criticized Branstad's record compared to Governor Ray's policies, trying to create a wedge between the popular governor and his lieutenant governor. Before a nonpartisan group, Conlin stated, "I'm running on my record. I think he (Branstad) should run on his, not from it. He voted 'no' on virtually every progressive proposal made by Governor Ray." She also lambasted Branstad for his votes and opposition on issues like the Iowa Equal Rights Amendment.

Branstad ran his campaign by emphasizing his ten years of experience in Iowa government and conveyed optimism about the condition of the state. He favored no additional taxation and instead opted to focus on eliminating government "waste" from the budget. Branstad said that one of his top priorities, if elected, was to set up a state loan program for students who were ineligible for federal loans. "If it hadn't been for a student loan, I wouldn't have been able to go to the University of Iowa," he said.

Branstad was also wholeheartedly against Conlin's $300 million bond proposal. He called the proposal an attempt at deficit spending—illegal under the state's constitution. To counter, he proposed an "Iowa fund" that would draw money from private investors to use in equity investing to provide capital for new start-up businesses. He campaigned to create 180,000 jobs through tax incentives and promised the state legislature could operate without any tax increases.

One of the few issues the candidates agreed upon was voiced during their October 29, 1982, debate. Jim Bittner (not part of the debates) and the Socialist Party were anxious to get to two percent of the vote during the general election. If accomplished, the Socialist Party would become a third party in Iowa, providing it with automatic ballot status. Bittner advocated that a moratorium of farm mortgage foreclosures should be enacted based on a petition that had been circulated by a Quad Cities group calling for the governor to immediately invoke the state of emergency. During a public debate, both Branstad and Conlin openly disagreed with this approach, stating that far too few farms were affected at the time. Branstad said only two percent of Iowa's farmers were currently in need of help.

On July 1, 1982, the campaign to replace Robert Ray as governor of Iowa changed dramatically. The tax returns promised by Roxanne Conlin during the primary campaign were completed and released by her staff. Her joint assets, consisting mostly of property in the Des Moines area with her husband, totaled more than $2.2 million. According to the tax returns, the Conlins paid $2,995 in federal taxes but nothing for state taxes on their joint return. James's company, Mid-Iowa Management Company, created the same tax shelters Roxanne Conlin had admonished others about during her campaign.

Until that day, Conlin had been leading in the polls, but the story destroyed her momentum. The Branstad campaign pounced on the opportunity, and the bumper sticker slogan "Taxanne" was born, based on a play-on-words from the popular 1978 song "Roxanne" performed by The Police. Conlin's lead of seven points in May quickly converted to a deficit. At that point, "the race was effectively over," wrote Strohman.[81]

Fisher agreed that this was the turning point. He owned a second home in Clear Lake, and once he boarded the Branstad express, he held annual fundraisers there for many years. "The summer during his first campaign for governor, I went to Mason City to find some people to help host the fundraiser and put it together, and I heard on the radio that Roxanne Conlin said she never paid any taxes. I thought, 'Wow! Did she really say that?' I remember I called Terry and said, 'We just won!'"[82]

Conlin's slide in the poll did not mean, however, the Branstad campaign didn't have its own setbacks. During the campaign, the Branstad team stated it planned to use his inauguration as an antiabortion fundraiser. Branstad made negative headlines by saying farmers were "greedy" and expressed his willingness to look into toll roads for the state. Although each statement was either taken out of context or retracted, the Conlin campaign made use of them.

By the end of fall, Branstad's lead had tightened, and both parties were anxious for a large voter turnout. On November 2, 1982, statewide participation was tremendous. At 5:00 p.m., Democratic Executive Director Michael Tramontina said he was "cautiously optimistic," because he received some indication that unemployed workers were turning out heavily. However, by 9:00 p.m. the mood of the Democratic Party on the Savery Hotel's sixth floor, where results were being tabulated, was subdued. By 10:30 p.m. Conlin emerged from her suite on the seventh floor of the same hotel to tell reporters she was conceding the race: "I've just called Terry and wished him my very best." During her concession speech a few minutes later, she expressed her "sincere wish that Terry succeed in his term as governor."

If the mood of excitement was totally vanquished in the Conlin camp, the opposite was true at the Des Moines Marriott where the newly elected governor was celebrating with friends and supporters. By 9:15 p.m., ABC News had declared Branstad the victor. A deafening roar awaited Branstad as he entered the packed room. A small aisle had to be physically created so Branstad, Robert Ray, and Senator Charles Grassley could make their way to the podium.

"The Republicans in this great state of Iowa proved again that we can do the job," said the state's youngest governor ever. "We've had fourteen years of great leadership from Bob Ray. We've established a tradition of progress, stability, and living within our means. The voters voted to stay on that course."

Echoing the sentiments expressed later by Fisher and Strohman, Democratic leaders saw the defeat largely as the result of Conlin's tax situation.

"Clearly, the tax issue hurt us more than we thought it would," said Democratic Party Chairman David Nagle. "I don't think Terry won because of his economic policies; he won because of Roxanne's tax issue." Former Democratic Governor Harold Hughes agreed. "Obviously, it was the tax thing that did the Conlin campaign in."[83]

In total, Branstad garnered 548,313 votes to Conlin's 483,291, giving Branstad a 6.3 percent margin of victory. Branstad may have won the election, but the Democrats succeeded in many other races. The election of lieutenant governor went to Democrat Bob Anderson over his Republican rival Lawrence E. Pope—only the third time in Iowa state political history that the governor and lieutenant governor were from two opposing parties.

Anderson's victory provided Democrats some degree of hope that Branstad's economic policies could be muffled by one of their own in his administration. During the campaigning in October, Branstad mentioned that if Anderson won, it could create a "dangerous situation," as the lieutenant governor presides over the Iowa Senate and is the one who usually pushes the governor's legislation. "If I found out he was trying to sabotage everything I did, I'd be reluctant to include him in my planning," he said.[84]

Although there was elation with the Branstad victory, some Republicans suggested he was elected primarily due to Ray's success and popularity. Some of the party leaders did not believe Branstad could adequately fill Ray's shoes. Tim Hyde, executive director of the state Republican Party, said, "I wouldn't want to be the newly elected governor right now. The governor-elect has to face some problems tougher than Governor Ray has had to face. These are tough times."[85]

What he did not fully realize was that Terry Branstad was very darn tough as well. Not only had he proven himself time after time—from the football fields at Forest City to rhetoric class at Iowa, to the political battles of the entire state—but he understood how to compete at the highest levels. His insatiable desire to become a major force in the state he loved, and the work ethic bestowed upon him by his parents, had enabled him to reach the top position in the entire state. A new era was dawning on the Iowa political scene, one that would be dominated by the former Leland lad for decades to come.

CHAPTER FIVE

Keeping His Job (The Election of 1986)

During his first term as governor, Branstad came face to face with one of the biggest issues he would encounter as governor, and it would allow him to show he was willing to compromise when the citizens of the state made their feelings known. In 1983, he had vetoed a bill for a state lottery. As a matter of principle, he didn't think gambling should be encouraged in Iowa. But the issue kept cropping up, and finally Branstad swallowed hard and signed it in April 1985. The lottery debuted on August 22, 1985, at the Iowa State Fair and was an instant success, selling over 6.4 million tickets its first week of operation.

"He was philosophically opposed to it because it's gambling and he didn't like it," said Lyle Simpson. "I told him the public wants it and it's going to happen over your dead body, so you might as well sign it. What you can do is allow it to happen and then regulate it, and that's what he did. We have one of the best gambling industries in the nation because of Terry Branstad."[86]

Almost three decades later, Branstad explained his decision and how he arrived at it. "In 1983, my first year in office, I supported pari-mutuel betting on horses. We have lots of people in Iowa who raise horses. I felt if we approved horse racing, then that would put the state in a position to regulate it. John Snackenberg of Irvington took me to see one of his horses race in South Dakota, and I became a supporter." He established a racing commission, and the Democratic legislature authorized both horse and dog racing, with tracks opening in Council Bluffs, Dubuque, Waterloo, and Prairie Meadows in Des Moines.

"The legislature went a step further and passed a state lottery—basically fleecing our own people is the way I looked at it," he said in 2014. "We already had bingo, so I vetoed the bill. The legislature passed it again in 1984, and I vetoed it again."[87]

There was a $50 million lottery in Illinois, and a great number of Iowans went across the Mississippi River to buy tickets there, spending hard-earned Iowa cash in a neighboring state. Because of his stance against the Iowa lottery, Branstad was booed at a Hawkeye football game and at a rodeo in Fort Madison.

Though not a gambler himself, Branstad reluctantly came to realize that "if the people of Iowa wanted it then I shouldn't stand in the way just because I didn't like it personally." As he contemplated adjusting his thinking on the matter, one of his main concerns was how to maintain the integrity of the system should he decide to sign the bill. He consulted with a man he admired, Dr. Ed Stanek, who had a PhD in physics, and then appointed him to run the lottery when Stanek "told me I would never have to worry about it."[88]

Stanek was true to his word. After earning a PhD in physics from Iowa State, he worked in state government for thirty-five years, primarily in the areas of energy and the environment. But Branstad recognized his ability to organize and run efficient groups and appointed him to the lottery post. Stanek ran the Iowa Lottery from 1985 until retiring in 2007, and in 2014 was presented with the Guy Simonis Lifetime Achievement Award by the World Lottery Association, the highest award given by the group, which represents ninety countries in the lottery industry.

Branstad signed the lottery into law in April 1985, and sales began on August 22, with a kickoff celebration at the Iowa State Fair. Some 6.4 million tickets were bought in the first week alone. At first, the profits were to go to a long-term economic program known as the Iowa Plan, but in 1992 the proceeds were switched to the state's general fund. According to the lottery website, "Today, lottery proceeds are used for three main purposes in Iowa. They provide support for veterans, help for a variety of significant programs through the state general fund, and (provide) backing for the Vision Iowa program."[89]

The website claims that by 2014, nearly $1.3 billion had been raised for state programs and more than $2.8 billion had gone to prizes for winning players. The state lottery has grown to the point where it employs 117 people across the state and sells its products at 2,500 retail locations.[90]

"It was a tough lesson for me," Branstad confided in 2014. "I've never bought a lottery ticket, but when I realized the majority of the people wanted it, I decided to go along. We had the fastest start-up of any lottery in the country, and it has never had an image problem. It's been well managed; I've never had to really worry about it."[91]

As many confidants would say through the years, Branstad was not an ideologue but was very pragmatic. One who can attest to that evaluation in regard to his positon on the lottery is Jeff Stein, who has a law degree and has covered Iowa politics and elections for newspapers, radio, and television outlets for thirty-five years, including Branstad's first run for governor in 1982.

"I recall Branstad's early opposition to gambling in Iowa, taking public stands against legalized gaming, including the state lottery," said Stein in 2014. "The idea gained popularity among members of the public, and it began to look like the governor was increasingly standing alone on the topic.

"In 1985, I was working for WSUI, the public radio station operated by the University of Iowa, and had scheduled an interview with the governor by telephone. His views against gambling were well known, but public polling and an informal survey of lawmakers suggested that a bill legalizing gaming would be passed that legislative session. I had an obligation to ask the 'gambling' question, despite knowing I would get the standard answer we had all heard before.

"But Branstad's answer shocked me. He said if the legislature passed a bill, since it was what the people of Iowa wanted, he would sign it. He spoke via speakerphone, with an aide in the room. I wasn't sure I heard him correctly, so I asked directly: 'So you're saying if the legislature passes a bill legalizing gambling, you'll sign it?'

"'That's what I've said,' he responded, 'because it's what Iowans want.'" Stein was so surprised by what had just transpired that after the interview ended, he asked his boss if he had ever heard the governor say he would sign a gambling bill. "He hadn't…nor had the Associated Press Des Moines bureau chief when I called him. The story quoting the governor ran statewide, and soon after, gambling was legal in Iowa.

"In hindsight, it was brilliant strategizing by the governor and his staff," said Stein. "If he had come out at his regular weekly news conference and said the same thing, it would have drawn major attention and accusations of flip-flopping. But by sliding the answer in during a phone interview with a radio station outside of Des Moines, the news was broken without the same attention as if he would have said it under the capitol dome. And if asked about it later, he could point to my interview (and perhaps others, with other individual stations) and say he had not changed his position at all, that he'd been saying he'd sign a bill for some time."[92]

The gambling issue resurfaced several times in the coming years. In the summer of 1988, it came to a head when David Yepsen reported, "Gov. Branstad said Tuesday he disagrees with a proposed plank in the Republican Party platform calling for elimination of the state lottery. GOP platform drafters are proposing that the 1988 Republican Party platform declare the state 'made a mistake by getting into the lottery business. We call for repeal of the Iowa lottery.'" Yepsen added that Branstad called the lottery pro-growth and pro-development and that he would continue to support it.[93] The repeal effort died, and the Iowa Lottery is now in its fourth decade.

On the domestic side, Chris Branstad was going through a major adjustment period as well at Terrace Hill. The move from an old farmhouse near Lake Mills to the luxurious mansion on the hill in the center of Des Moines seemed almost as if taken from a book on fairy tales. There were marble fireplaces, crystal chandeliers, ornate bookcases, winding stairways, massive wall carvings, lovely statues, and even velvet ropes to keep tourists from wandering into closed-off areas reserved for family.

As if that were not enough, she had to get used to the fact that she had a cook on the week days, a maid to help keep everything in place, access to a driver to take her shopping, if that was her desire, and a personal secretary to help with her schedule. As the young and attractive First Lady of the State of Iowa, Chris Branstad was constantly fielding requests for appearances, mostly for charitable causes, and was expected to maintain a very positive public image. She admitted it was all downright scary at first.

Carol Tjernagle was her personal assistant and helped her with the planning of state dinners, making sure that protocol was carried out, and handling her correspondence. But it was Chris Branstad who set the tone for the lifestyle that would be acceptable to her in the mansion on the hill. She made sure the kids were involved in public functions only when they wanted to be. Early on, she declined to buy a new designer dress suggested by a Des Moines insider, saying they were not wealthy and she simply could not afford it.

"If there are expectations Iowans put on their 'first family,' Chris Branstad doesn't seem to be looking for them," wrote Susan Weaver on April 3, 1983. "She says she intends to be herself and hopes Iowans will accept her that way."[94]

In 1984, Terry Branstad had the opportunity to take a short trip on Air Force One—the only time he has ever done so. President Reagan had come to Iowa for an event, and several members of Branstad's team were invited to fly from Waterloo to Des Moines. Even though Branstad regarded Reagan as his political idol, he didn't always agree with everything the Illinois-born president tried to do during his eight years in the Oval Office.

As his first term was winding down, Governor Branstad could look back with pride on his efforts (with the legislature) to reorganize much of state government, balance the budget, and stabilize the economy. But he entered the 1986 election cycle in a precarious situation because of the continued farm crisis. A 1986 survey of 1,040 Iowa farm families showed significant associations between the levels of financial distress, the perceived level of personal and family stress, and a deterioration in the life situations of those families. That situation provided many similarities in the rhetoric from the 1982 gubernatorial election and the 1986 campaign for the state's highest office.

Governor Branstad ran unopposed during the Republican primary and didn't officially start his reelection bid until March 21,

1986. The Democrats offered four candidates for their primary election, which started eighteen months before the election. They were sure they could unseat the governor based on a referendum of his first term in office.

The first Democrat in the primary was forty-two-year-old Lowell Junkins from the southeast Iowa town of Montrose. After graduating from Central Lee Community High School in Argyle, he attended Iowa State University and went on to become the mayor of his hometown. Junkins was elected to the Iowa State Senate in 1972 and reelected in each subsequent election. He served as minority leader of the senate from 1979 to 1981 and was elected majority leader in 1983. He resigned from his position in the senate in the fall of 1985 to concentrate on his quest to become governor. His campaign officially kicked off on March 10, 1985. At that event Junkins told the media, "The governor has charted no course for Iowa's future."[95]

His overall campaign strategy was based on a plan to rejuvenate the sluggish Iowa economy during the farm crisis by offering a similar (but larger) bond and tax plan as Roxanne Conlin had four years earlier. According to his plan, Junkins would jump-start the economy by selling $500 million worth of bonds compared to Conlin's $300 million proposal. He also campaigned that another $1 billion over a ten-year period would be generated through tax and spending changes.

He defended his plan against criticism by citing other states that had successfully done the same thing. He said, "We have a governor who sends a mixed signal by his own contradictory actions. First of all, he asks the federal government to invest in Iowa by loaning us money to help reestablish an economic base in our agricultural sector but lacking the courage himself. He criticizes me for asking Iowans to have the confidence to invest in Iowa. It is clearly a lack of leadership that leads to these contradictory actions."[96]

The second challenger was Lieutenant Governor Robert Anderson of Newton. Anderson was born in Marshalltown and earned his BA and MA from the University of Iowa. In 1974, while working as a teacher, he was elected to the Iowa House of Representatives. There, he rose in rank and became part of the Democratic leadership. In eight years he served on two-thirds of the standing committees in the house. In 1982, Anderson successfully won the elected office of lieutenant governor, replacing Branstad. Having won a statewide campaign, Anderson's name recognition was a positive.

The third candidate, state senator and golf store proprietor George Kinley, was a late entry into the race. Representing the south side of Des Moines, Kinley was first elected to the Iowa House in 1972, and then to the Iowa Senate in 1974. Kinley was opposed to Junkins's plan and instead called for increasing the state sales tax to 5 percent for four years, using the new revenue to pay down the state's $200 million debt.

The fourth and final Democratic candidate for the office of governor was Clinton E. Berryhill of Readlyn, a small town in northeast Iowa. Berryhill filed his nomination the same day Junkins entered the race and was not considered a major contestant in the primary.

On the June 3, 1986, primary election, Junkins garnered 70,605 votes, or 53 percent of the vote. Anderson ended with 44,550 votes; Kinley earned 15,473 votes;, and Berryhill only mustered 3,503. Junkins's decision to step down as the state senate's majority leader paid dividends when both Kinley and Anderson were mired in a legislative session that lasted until its adjournment in May 1986.

Although Governor Branstad headed President Ronald Reagan's 1984 presidential reelection in the state of Iowa, Branstad distanced himself from the nation's chief executive because of his belief the federal government wasn't doing enough to stem the farm crisis. Branstad also believed his "slow-but-steady" approach to jump-starting the state's economy was working but required patience.

The precursors of the farm crisis of the 1980s had begun the decade before. It was a perfect storm of failed policy, global economics and politics, and the drastic fluctuation in land and commodity prices—along with two droughts. The result of all that was the worst economic landscape for American farmers since the Great Depression of the 1930s. But unlike that depression, where the collective population of the country faced a decimated economy and uncertainty, only the agriculture industry felt the brute force of this 1980s crisis.

The agriculture industry, like most others, had felt the positive effect of technology following World War II. With the advent of new machinery, seed, fertilizers, and pesticides, farmers were able to obtain record yields from the rich Iowa farmland. The most common problem was an abundance of crops keeping prices down. That changed during the early 1970s when weather outside the United States made for poor harvests around the world. Suddenly, surpluses dwindled and prices rose.

The Nixon administration and the Soviet Union negotiated a multiyear contract for wheat and feed grains in 1972. For Iowa farmers, corn prices tripled in only two years, and for the first time since record keeping began, per capita farm income actually exceeded that of urban Americans. In 1973, President Nixon's secretary of agriculture, Earl Butz, responded by calling upon American farmers to plant "fencerow to fencerow," and he told them "to get big or get out." Farmers took these words to heart, and production boomed.

The spike in prices for commodities was a blessing for farmers but was short lived. In 1979, the new Federal Reserve chairman, Paul Volcker, raised interest rates to stem inflation. Interest rates ballooned from single digits to double digits, a situation that had not been seen since the Civil War. Rates hit a record 21.5 percent in 1981. The Fed's actions made the cost of borrowing money prohibitive for all Americans but devastated family farms in Iowa and across the United States. The problems for Iowa producers compounded with global politics. In 1979, the Soviet Union invaded Afghanistan, and in response, President Jimmy Carter ordered a cease of commodity exports to the US's Cold War adversary.

The result was an excess surplus that pushed prices down and rising interest rates that caused many farmers to take on more debt. These high interest rates were not covered by the returns on harvest, yet many producers were borrowing more in hopes that better crops and higher prices would come.

By the summer of 1984, the plight of Iowa farmers was at a fever pitch. Most agriculture-rich states looked to the federal government for help, but their pleas fell on deaf ears. David Stockman, director of the Office of Management and Budget during President

Ronald Reagan's first term, argued that the agriculture industry had caused its own problems and the federal government should not be involved.

In January 1985, Tom Huston, Iowa's superintendent of banking, and some top state officials and experts—including Governor Branstad and Neil Harl, an Iowa State University economist—attended a meeting at the White House with Stockman. The delegation was there to call on the Reagan administration to make good on a campaign promise for $650 million in credit relief for Midwestern farmers.

"He (Stockman) came in late, and almost before he got settled into his chair, he started talking and being critical of the fact that agriculture had caused its own problem," said Harl. "At one point, there was an exchange between Branstad and Stockman, with Branstad getting up and grabbing his chair and slamming it down for emphasis and said, 'I chaired the Reagan committee for reelection in Iowa, I think I deserve better treatment than this.'"[97]

The trauma of the farm crisis was felt by Branstad both as the leader of a state whose future is heavily dependent on agriculture and on a personal level. He had invested heavily in farmland himself, buying at a time when prices were at a peak.

"He was suffering just like everyone else," said Doug Gross, who served as his chief of staff at the time. "He had bought land in 1981 at the top of the market and had lost heavily. In fact, I believe he had every right to declare bankruptcy, but he steadfastly refused to do so. He thought it would set a bad example for others who were suffering." Gross paused, reflecting back on the moment. "He's a man of great integrity. He simply wouldn't back down. He felt he should go through what other farmers were experiencing."[98]

To this day, Branstad has a sign on his desk that was given to him during the farm crisis. It reads: "Tough times don't last but tough people do." In 2014, he pointed to the sign with pride, explaining that it was the title of a book written by Robert Schuler, a native of Alton, Iowa, who created the popular "Hour of Power" television ministry from the Crystal Cathedral Church in Garden Grove, California.

Branstad led the state drive to help ease the burden of the farm crisis. His administration rolled back property taxes on producers so their livestock and farm equipment would be exempt. In 1985, the state established the Iowa Rural Concern Hotline, connecting rural families and communities with a range of services from financial and legal to mental health.

The state also arranged for farmer–lender mediation to assist both parties in finding common ground to resolve the crisis. The governor imposed a partial farm foreclosure moratorium that prevented foreclosure if a farmer paid the interest but was not current on the principal of his or her mortgage.

The Agricultural Credit Act of 1987 was passed by the federal government and enacted on January 6, 1988. The act authorized $4 billion in financial assistance to struggling farmers and related industries. The act set new guidelines for those who borrowed from Farm Credit Services or the Farmers Home Administration. By late 1988, the average farmland price rose 20 percent over the previous year and commodity prices increased, signaling the beginning of the end to the farm crisis in Iowa and across the country.

It was apparent that the actions of Governor Branstad had helped create the change for Iowa and the entire nation. The Iowa farm crisis was finally over, and land values began to climb upward once again. After that, Iowa farmland values increased for nearly twenty-six straight years, until the federal EPA proposed reducing the renewable fuel standard in the fall of 2013. Since then, Iowa farmland values have decreased by 15 percent.

"Fifty-eight percent of Iowans say they approve of the job Branstad is doing—virtually unchanged from the ratings the Republican governor has received over the last two years," wrote Kenneth Pins in the *Des Moines Register* on June 27, 1988. "One sign of new life in Branstad's rating is his standing with farmers, who have taken a much brighter view of elected officials in general in 1988's improved economic climate. Three of four farmers now say they approved of Branstad's work."[99]

However, running in 1986 for a second term, Governor Branstad campaigned on a three-part plan for Iowans that concentrated on the state's economy. Improving the business climate, aggressively promoting economic growth, and the marketing and promotion of the state through tourism were his top priorities. In addition, the governor campaigned to effectively utilize the $125 million to $175 million in new revenue generated by the Tax Reform Act of 1986 that passed Congress and was signed by President Reagan that year.

Junkins contended that if Republicans were elected or reelected in 1986 then farmers would see no change in policy and the farm crisis would continue. Junkins also cited a source that said that Iowa ranked forty-eighth in the nation for job creation. On September 30, 1985, Junkins introduced a plan to support small businesses of Iowa with $100 million in aid. He said the funds would be applied for better job training, a series of loan and insurance programs, and more research and incubation of new businesses. This plan was part of his overall $500 million bond and tax package devised to jolt the Iowa economy and displace the incumbent governor.

"Some of these programs have already been put in place, and they're good ideas," said Junkins at the unveiling. But, he added, "They're not big enough to turn the economy around."[100]

Governor Branstad's team countered effectively. "These programs were all started under the Branstad administration," said spokesman Dick Vohs. "The only thing new about them is that Junkins would use debt and higher taxes to pay for them. Higher taxes is not what small business needs."[101]

Using the bond issue to its advantage, the Branstad campaign created a new bumper sticker theme for the opposition's plan. It was labelled the "Junkins' Junk Bond Plan." This campaign also marked the second alliance with a political adviser who was destined to become one of the most influential figures in recent history. Branstad hired Roger Ailes to help him plan his strategy in 1986 and went back to him again in 1990.

A graduate of Ohio University, Ailes was a media consultant for presidents Richard Nixon, Ronald Reagan, and George H. W. Bush and many other notables. He made his reputation via his ability to help educate his clients in ways that made them more appealing to the voters. After leaving the consulting business in 1992, Ailes moved into the television business and became president of Fox News Channel and chairman of the Fox Television Stations Group and, hence, one of the most powerful people in all of politics. Along the way he helped shape the careers of such people as Rush Limbaugh, Sean Hannity, and Bill O'Reilly, to name just a few.

But he also drew fire from Democratic operatives, who called Ailes's style mostly negative.

"I believe in hiring people who are skilled and effective in doing what they do, and Roger Ailes is the best media consultant in the country," said Branstad at the time. Years later, he explained the way Ailes worked: "I went into his office in New York City, and he gave me a pepper drill . . . meaning he would pepper someone with questions then stop and freeze-frame it and go over it with you, even discussing how you use your hands and things like that. It was quite an experience, and I learned a lot from it."[102]

Three debates were held before the election. Junkins pushed for more debates, but Governor Branstad maintained that any more would dilute the process and that less of the populace would pay attention. At the end of the campaign, the Associated Press reported the two were "bickering about religion, abortion and who had the most attractive wife." The report about the candidates' wives stemmed from a Branstad campaign stop in Ida Grove, where he referred to his three debates with Junkins.

"I feel we did well in those debates. I know my wife looked better than the wife of . . ." Branstad said, pausing and not completing the sentence. "Well, let's put it this way: She's the best-looking first lady and the youngest first lady in the United States of America. I won't say who she's better than. I'll just say she's the best. That should keep me out of trouble."[103]

There was another element to the debates that few knew about, recalled Susan Neely, who was in charge of the 1986 campaign.

"For debates in both the 1982 and 1986 campaigns, it became our tradition that I would represent Terry in the coin toss to determine the order for opening statements. I had an unbroken string and won the coin toss every single time. I'm not particularly superstitious, but I was relieved when I won the toss for the last debate in 1986, considering a good omen for the outcome of the election."[104]

Neely confided that in both campaigns she had to contend with a slight problem of the governor, one that had to do with bumper stickers.

"Terry isn't high maintenance in any appreciable way. However, he did have a fixation on making sure that a maximum number of cars had blue-and-white bumper stickers. If he pulled into a fund-raiser and wasn't greeted by a squad of eager young people ready to affix bumper stickers, it didn't matter how much money was raised. He believed the event wasn't a success. Early on in this campaign, I tried to argue that it wasn't always necessary to involve young people in bumper branding, and, in fact, sometimes major donors don't even want a bumper sticker. He disabused me of this notion, pointing out that every time he sees a bumper sticker, he knows it's a vote!"[105]

Leading up to the November 4 election, most polls showed Branstad with a shrinking lead. In total, the candidates vying for the office of governor spent a record $3 million. Branstad spent $1,878,910 to Junkins's $997,167. Predicting a forty-year low in voter turnout, both the Democrats and Republicans urged their constituents to exercise their vote. A *Des Moines Register* poll on Sunday, November 2, 1986, showed Junkins had gained ground the two weeks prior. The poll said that a lead of 18 percent in favor of the governor on October 18 had shrunk to 8 percent, with 12 percent undecided.

The day before the election, Governor Branstad campaigned with fellow Republican candidates at Oelwein, Dubuque, Mason City, Burlington, and Ottumwa. Junkins ended his campaign at the Des Moines' Alternative High School—the same site where he announced his candidacy. On Election Day, a total of 910,623 votes were cast, and Governor Branstad garnered 472,712 (52 percent) to 436,987 (48 percent) votes for Junkins.

In his concession speech, Junkins said there was reason to be optimistic about his campaign. "In my defeat good things have happened in Iowa. There is now a commitment to education, jobs, and agriculture that wasn't there a few months ago."[106]

Branstad's victory party, which was again held at the Des Moines Marriott Hotel, was led with chants of "four more years" from a group of approximately four hundred people. During his victory speech, Branstad shared his appreciation for the people of Iowa along with optimism about the state's future. "Most of all, I'm proud of the people in this state. I know what they've gone through, and we've already planted the seeds to diversify this state's economy."

Iowa Republican Party chairman David Oman wasn't surprised at how close the race turned out to be. "Everyone knew the Democrats would come home in the last few days," he said. "We knew it would be close, (but) not quite this close."[107]

The talk among Democrats following their defeat was not fueled by a referendum on the philosophical differences in the vision of Iowa—mostly the proposed $500 million bond issue by Junkins versus a conservative approach by Governor Branstad. Junkins gave the governor a good run, said Democratic Party chairman Arthur Davis. "It's (Branstad's win) not hard to understand. It's hard to beat Republican incumbents in Iowa. In conservative societies like Iowa, the populace becomes afraid that things could get worse."[108]

Strohman, in his 2014 article in *CityView*, had a somewhat different take: "Anderson likely would have run well against Branstad, particularly after having already won a statewide race, but the Democrats chose Junkins, who represented the party insiders and espoused their same failed message."[109]

In the race for lieutenant governor, Iowans elected the first woman to the office. The presiding lieutenant governor, Bob Anderson, had resigned so he could concentrate on his own quest for the office of governor, opening up the spot, and Democrat Jo Ann Zimmerman narrowly won over her Republican challenger, Joan Lipsky. It was the second consecutive Iowa gubernatorial election where the lieutenant governor and governor were from opposing parties, and it would be the last.

The 1986 gubernatorial election was a referendum on Governor Branstad's first term in office. In the end, Branstad's slow-but-steady approach to fix the economy was chosen over a half-billion-dollar proposal based on new bond and tax policies. Branstad had survived the tightest gubernatorial race that he would encounter during his six campaigns for Iowa's highest office.

In his inaugural address on January 21, 1987, Branstad shifted his primary emphasis to education. He called for an extra $151 million investment in that area, pushing for what he called "a program of unprecedented scope and direction in education."

"There are those who say we cannot afford to make this commitment," he said. "Let us not forget that the one thing more expensive than education is ignorance."

CHAPTER SIX

Going for a Third Term (The Election of 1990)

In his column in the *Des Moines Register* on October 2, 1988, editor James P. Gannon offered his opinion on "how to fix what's wrong with Iowa." He said that the focus should be on the state's economic future, stating that Iowa "suffered a dreadful economic beating in the 1980s" and "the campaign should focus on making the next decade a much better one for Iowans than the past decade.

"Branstad had the misfortune of coming into office when powerful economic forces had gathered to deal Iowa's farms, small businesses and small towns a series of hard blows. That he has survived this decade politically to seek a third term in 1990 is a measure of his adroitness as a campaigner and to his luck in drawing poor opponents. He may not have the luck of facing a pushover next time, but he might benefit from a better economic climate. Iowa's farms and businesses are on the mend now, and 1988 is turning out to be a good year for most, despite the drought."[110]

Gannon believed it was essential that the state deal with population decline and create a vision that would enhance its appeal to young people as a desirable place to live, do business, and raise a family.

Near the end of his second term, Branstad emerged as a forceful player on the national Republican scene. He was well known and respected in the Reagan White House, due in large part to Reagan's strong connection to Des Moines from his years (1936–37) at WHO Radio, and Branstad's work ethic and integrity. In 1989, he was elected to a one-year term as chair of the National Governors Association and also served as chair of the Midwestern Governors

Association. He flew to Washington, DC, numerous times for various meetings and was sought out by Republicans to give campaign speeches and statements of support.

In announcing his plans as chairman of the national group, Branstad said he would focus on education and the environment: "It's an opportunity to get national and international exposure for the quality of Iowa education," he told Thomas Fogarty of the *Des Moines Register*, "and for some of the innovative things we've done in the environmental area. I think that helps our overall efforts of economic development."[111]

Robert Behn, a scholar at Duke University who is director of the Governors Center there, predicted the chairmanship would benefit Branstad in the 1990 election. "It's got to be a political plus, if only to the extent that it says this governor's colleagues think enough of him to make him chairman."[112]

Shortly after, Branstad was one of a small group of governors selected to meet with British Prime Minister Margaret Thatcher at the United Nations, adding to his growing reputation.

One of his most interesting trips came several months earlier, on November 22, 1988, when he visited the USS *Lexington* while attending a National Republican Governors Conference in Point Clear, Alabama. The aircraft carrier was on a training mission in the Gulf of Mexico, and the governors were invited to land on the aircraft carrier. Unbeknownst to Branstad at the time, the USS *Lexington* was the final home of Nile Kinnick, Iowa's legendary football player and 1939 Heisman Trophy winner. Kinnick was stationed on the ship when he made his fatal flight from its deck on the morning of June 2, 1943, off the coast of South America. His Wildcat 4F4 single-seat plane developed an oil leak and went down in calm waters several miles from the ship. Though rescue planes and boats were sent out immediately, Kinnick's plane was never found. He was just twenty-four at the time of his death. Kinnick's paternal grandfather, George W. Clarke, was a two-term Iowa governor (1913–1917), and a bust of Governor Clarke sits behind Governor Branstad's desk in his office in the state capitol. Many who knew Nile Kinnick felt confident he would someday run for governor of Iowa.

A few months later, Branstad found himself on the receiving end of a congratulatory opinion piece that appeared in the *Mason City Globe-Gazette*, regarding his efforts in pushing education reform all across the nation. The headline read "Branstad makes education No. 1."

"Gov. Terry Branstad has done the remarkable in his short tenure as chairman of the National Governor's Conference: The Iowa Republican has convinced the President of the United States to convene with the 50 governors for an education summit today—and they're all showing up. This is only the third time in history that the President has met with the governors (Teddy Roosevelt was there for the first meeting, and Franklin Roosevelt attended during the depths of the Great Depression). This fact underscores the urgency with which the nation views its educational situation, and it is a natural function of a chairman from Iowa.

"Branstad cautions that we should not expect too much in the way of grand plans or specifics. Rather, the several closed-door meetings are designed to bring education to the nation's forefront. That task may already have been accomplished, by virtue of the President's attendance. Other governors certainly will press for specific commitments to new programs, and observers are monitoring closely for such (witness the op-ed article on this page and Gov. Mario Cuomo's incantations in the *Globe-Gazette* Tuesday).

"Branstad ought to be prepared to deal with some nuts-and-bolts proposals. As chairman, he may have to stand on those planks when he comes back to Iowa—whether merited or not. But platforms and the dreams on which they're built come and go. Whatever happens, or doesn't happen, at the education summit this week, Iowans should be gratified that the issue they hold so dear has been brought emphatically to the nation's attention by our governor.

"That is no small accomplishment."[113]

Looking ahead to 1990, Branstad seemed to be in a good position to secure a third term. David Yepsen, perhaps the state's best known political writer of the past three decades, predicted in a column on May 30, 1988, that Branstad was going to triumph again. "The bet now has to be that Terry Branstad will get re-elected to the governorship in 1990. He's doing a smoother job, the economy is moving his way and the Democrats look to be giving him a free ride."

Yepsen even went so far as to make a rather surprising comparison between Branstad and his old boss and predecessor. "Branstad is probably a better governor than Bob Ray was. It has to have been easier for Ray to be governor in the boom times of the '70s than for Branstad to try to manage the state during the grime times of the '80s. Ray had it so good that any tough decisions—like closing rinky-dink schools or ending duplication at state universities—could be postponed.

"For Branstad, the decisions have been far different. There have been tax increases and budget cuts. Ray certainly did his work with more social polish than Branstad shows, but it's clear that Terry Branstad's times and choices are far more difficult to manage than Ray's."[114]

The election of 1990 had a different look with the dissolution of a statewide race to decide the office of lieutenant governor. An amendment to the Iowa Constitution in the fall of 1988 meant that for the first time nominees of their respective parties for the office of governor would choose their running mates instead of the office holder elected in a statewide election. Branstad had pushed for such a bill. "Much of the impetus for the concept has come because Republican Branstad has had a Democratic lieutenant governor since he was first elected in 1982," reported the Associated Press. "Critics said that made little sense because a Democratic lieutenant governor won't have much to do under a Republican administration. The only formal role of the lieutenant governor is to preside over the senate, where virtually all real decisions are made by the floor leaders."[115]

But for Governor Branstad's third campaign during the primary season, things looked the same when again no fellow Republicans challenged the incumbent for the nomination. However, there had been talk of a possible challenge, and from an unexpected source.

"Gov. Terry Branstad scorned suggestions Monday he faces an intraparty challenge from U.S. Sen. Charles Grassley, insisting it's too early to talk about 1990 gubernatorial politics," wrote Kevin Baskins of the *Des Moines Register* in 1989. "Reports have surfaced during the past week that Grassley, who won a landslide victory last year for a second six-year term, might be interested in running for governor. The speculation has been fueled by criticism Branstad has gotten from the right wing of his own party.

"Branstad got himself in political hot water with the conservative wing of the Republican Party when he called for a major restructuring of Iowa's income tax code."[116]

The article, which also included work by the Associated Press, quoted both Branstad and Grassley as denying there was much chance that Grassley would make a move in that direction, and the rumors soon faded away.

Terry Branstad had to deal with a severe personal loss on April 5, 1990, when his mother died of a heart attack at age sixty-four. He flew to Forest City when he received word that she had been taken by ambulance to the local hospital.

"She'd always have people in stitches," the governor told Art Cullen, writer for the *Forest City Summit.* "We used to argue about politics a lot, too." Cullen added that Rita Branstad "was a longtime member of the Winnebago County Democratic Central Committee but was converted to the GOP when Terry entered politics. She was a tireless campaigner . . . hauling a trailer around back roads with a huge Branstad sign."[117]

But it was soon back to work. The Democratic primary for governor saw five candidates vie for the right to face Branstad in the general election. Donald "Don" D. Avenson was a long-term member of the Iowa House of Representatives. Originally from Minneapolis and a high school graduate from Oelwein, Avenson continued his post-secondary studies at the University of Wisconsin at River Falls and earned degrees in both political science and history. Avenson was first elected to the Iowa House in 1972. In his second term he became assistant house majority leader and held that position until 1978. From 1979 to 1982, Avenson served as house minority leader until becoming the speaker of the Iowa House in 1983, and he continued in that capacity through the 1990 gubernatorial election.

Tom Miller, originally from Dubuque and a Wahlert High School graduate, received a bachelor's degree from Loras College.

He went on to earn his JD from Harvard Law School in 1969. Miller was elected as Iowa's attorney general in 1978 and held that position until he threw his hat in the gubernatorial primary in 1990.

The third primary candidate was Jo Ann (McIntosh) Zimmerman, who was born in Van Buren County and graduated as valedictorian of Keosauqua High School. She entered the Broadlawns Hospital School of Nursing and earned her bachelor's degree. Zimmerman was elected to the Iowa House in 1982. In 1986, she won the office of lieutenant governor.

The fourth candidate was John Chrystal, a farmer, banker, Democratic Party leader, adviser, and citizen ambassador to the Soviet Union from Coon Rapids. Chrystal first gained notoriety when, as a member of the Garst family, he helped host Russian Premier Nikita Khrushchev on a tour of his farming operation in 1958.

Darold Powers, an activist from Des Moines, also threw his hat in the ring. Powers was proposing a twenty-year plan for building a new state infrastructure. In a campaign speech in Spencer he said, "This is the first year I've ever done anything like this. I'm the rookie."[118]

David Yepsen, in his *Des Moines Register* column of May 30, 1988, had predicted a relatively easy path to a three-peat for Branstad: "The economy is getting better and the Democrats are headed toward a five-way primary fight that will leave them divided and broke. Another reason to bet on Branstad is the Democrats' decision to kid glove him." Yepsen made the point that it appeared as though the Democrats had indicated they would not use negative campaigning techniques, which Yepsen said were effective. "As Bob Dole learned in New Hampshire this year from George Bush, you can't let attacks go unanswered. Terry Branstad uses the same media consultant as Bush: a guy named Roger Ailes, who is one of the best in the business."[119]

A major issue in the Democratic primary was the overriding topic of abortion. Of the five Democratic candidates, Tom Miller was the only one who spoke out against abortion. A *Des Moines Register* poll conducted April 16–18, 1990, showed the attorney general with 21 percent, Avenson with 18 percent, and Chrystal with

14 percent. Miller began to be hammered by the National Abortion Rights Action League and other abortion rights supporters even though he made a repeated campaign promise that he would not advocate or propose any new restrictions, with the exception of parental notification for minors with the appropriate safeguards.

In a *New York Times* article of May 28, it was reported that Amy Maxey, a retired associate professor of sociology who held an abortion rights party in her Sioux City home, said: "I come awfully close to being willing to vote single issue, although generally I would deplore that. I think this is a critical time for us."[120]

Being in favor of abortion rights didn't make a candidate immune to attacks. Many abortion rights groups feared a threat of splitting the vote between the two leading pro-choice candidates, so they consolidated their efforts for Avenson over Chrystal, prompting the latter to complain about "tin-horn, would-be kingmakers from Washington" influencing the race in Iowa.[121]

Avenson said he was convinced the abortion issue would be a key to a primary win, stating that it was what created the most emotion among the primary voters.

As the primary election approached, Zimmerman dropped out and became Avenson's running mate. The primary elections took place on June 5, 1990. Avenson collected 79,022 votes, or 39 percent; Chrystal ended with 63,364 votes, or 31 percent; and Miller had 52,170 votes, or 26 percent of the votes.

For his part, Branstad commented that he was not at all surprised by Avenson's win, saying he got all the traditional groups behind him. The governor also said he doubted abortion would be a major factor in the election. Speaking on the Iowa Press program on Iowa Public Television, he said, "It's an issue, and I don't think it should be avoided. It's not the only issue. There are many other issues that are important." He added, "I'm not afraid of it . . . (but the voters) recognize that being a governor is a lot more than where you stand on abortion."

All three of the top candidates in the Democratic primary immediately asked their supporters to unite behind Avenson. "I'll do anything I can to help win this campaign, to win the governor's race," said Miller. "This is the end of one campaign but the beginning of another."[122]

The main issues surrounding the 1990 general election campaign included education, economic development, capital punishment, and taxes. The two candidates clearly differed from one another on almost all views. Avenson campaigned for a "limited tuition increase" for college students and wanted to eliminate tuition at community colleges when state revenues allowed for it. Branstad focused more on K-12 teachers and aimed to raise their salaries to the national average during his next four years. Avenson championed economic development through state assistance with job training. Branstad, at the helm of an economy that was steadily gaining back ground from the devastating 1980s farm crisis, pushed a larger vision. The governor chose a strategy to "strengthen and diversify" the state economy. He campaigned to implement a program to encourage foreign governments to invest in Iowa.

His campaign ad stated that he had saved Iowa $60 million by downsizing and reorganizing government, had rejected $277 million in tax increases and $358 million in extra spending, and had maintained a balanced budget every year he was in office. While Branstad was stressing that "education is the cornerstone of a dynamic state and healthy economy," the overall theme for the Republican ticket was "Dare to dream of an even better Iowa."

The topic of abortion, which had nearly created a single-issue primary focus for the Democrats, did resurface in the general election. Avenson was pro-choice and intended to veto any new restrictions passed by the legislature. He was opposed to the state having any power to restrict a woman's right to choose. Branstad, a pro-life advocate, campaigned to not revise the existing state regulations on abortion. However, the governor said he was willing to sign parental notification and statistical reporting bills if they passed through the legislature.

Regarding capital punishment, Avenson opposed reinstating the death penalty but campaigned to make drug dealers "look over their shoulder every day." Branstad favored reinstatement of capital punishment for criminals who committed murder to cover up another capital offense and for inmates who killed prison guards while serving a sentence of life in prison.

The one topic the candidates agreed upon was taxes: Branstad and Avenson both felt that no tax increases would need to be implemented during the upcoming year.

On June 11, 1990, the Branstad campaign picked up a significant endorsement from a union that traditionally (and for his first two gubernatorial elections) sided with the Democratic Party. The state's teachers union, the Iowa State Education Association, endorsed Branstad over Avenson for the general election. The union had endorsed Avenson during the Democratic primary. However, Ken Tilp, the president of the union, recognized Governor Branstad's record since his reelection in 1986 of including a $92.5 million increase in teacher pay in 1987.

"In 1986, he (Branstad) didn't have credibility with us. In the last four years, he has become credible." The last time the union had supported a Republican candidate for governor was Robert Ray in 1974.[123]

With the amendment to the Iowa Constitution in 1986 allowing the candidates for governor to pick their own running mates (instead of the office being elected in a statewide ballot), Branstad announced that Joy Corning would be his partner on the ticket. Corning was born in Bridgewater, a small town in south central Iowa, and was a graduate of the University of Northern Iowa. She was a former teacher, member of the Cedar Falls school board, former director of the Iowa Association of School Boards, and was presently serving her second four-year term as a state senator, representing what was then Senate District 12 in Black Hawk County. Her pro-choice stance on abortion balanced the ticket by differing with the governor's view but helped to mitigate the topic during the general election.

Corning was in the senate when the law was changed to make it possible for candidates for governor and lieutenant governor to be from the same party. "But I never thought it would apply to me," she said in 2014, adding that she was surprised when her name first appeared in a newspaper as a possible candidate for the second spot on the ticket. She was invited to meet with Branstad and told him she was interested in being considered, then met with the governor's staff. Shortly after, she and her husband, Burt, had breakfast at Terrace Hill with Terry and Chris Branstad. "Burt and I discussed the possibility and how much it could change our lives," she said. Then came the word that she was Branstad's choice for lieutenant governor.

"There was some opposition at the state convention," she recalled. "When someone asked Terry why he picked Joy Corning, he said it was because I had won elections and knew how to campaign. But I think he realized I had an even temperament and was strongly in the middle. I was thrilled to be picked—it opened up a whole new world for me, after eleven years on the Cedar Falls school board and being in my second terms as a state senator."[124]

In selecting a woman who wasn't always in lockstep with him, Branstad showed that he was capable of working with differing viewpoints and believed in diversity at the highest levels of government.

"Joy and I don't agree on every issue," said the governor at the time. "I don't think there are great disagreements. On the vast majority of critical issues facing the state, we are in tune. Our basic approach and philosophy are in line."[125] They were also in synch with their work ethic; Corning estimates that she travelled over twenty thousand miles around the state in the time between being selected as Branstad's running mate in mid-June and the election in early November.

Her administrative assistant, Carol Zeigler, did most of the driving while Joy studied the issues she would be discussing at the next stop. Two of her top concerns were foster care programs and diversity.

A key moment in the campaign occurred when a farm couple declared at a town meeting in Oelwein that they were going to lose their farm due to hangover issues from the farm crisis. They said they had contacted Avenson's office and weren't offered any help. Branstad's campaign people heard of their plight and worked to have the mortgage restructured. Consultant Roger Ailes arranged for the Oelwein couple to be interviewed on how Branstad had helped save their farm.

David Roederer, campaign manager at the time, recalled in 2015 that it was the turning point in the campaign and that the episode was a perfect example of how well the Branstad staff worked together for a common goal. He related that Keith Heffernan, a staff worker, received a call "from someone who had contacted the Avenson office to tell them of the situation but had been told 'we don't do stuff like that.'"

The Branstad staff took the ball and ran with it, and the governor was supportive all the way. "The wife wound up doing a testimonial for us, and it spoke volumes about the kind of people the governor employs," said Roederer. He told of another time when the governor impressed even a veteran reporter with his ability to mingle with the folks at every level.

"Mike Glover of the AP took his daughter to the Tulip Festival in Pella as a family outing. The governor had put on a costume, wooden shoes and all, and was helping clean the streets. The following week Glover told me, 'Your guy will never get beat. I saw the governor cleaning the streets in Pella, and I thought to myself there are probably a few other politicians who would do that, but none would enjoy doing it like Terry Branstad.'"

Roederer couldn't resist a chuckle while retelling the story. "How many politicians would do that? The thing is, people relate so well to him because they see how genuine he is and that he really cares."[126]

Avenson believed that Branstad was going to make the charge that he was a bully, so his first television ad explained that he was not a bully. But the label stuck that Avenson was a bully even though the Branstad campaign had no intention of making such a claim. "The bully charge backfired," said Branstad in 2014. "Avenson was a very powerful insider in political circles, but he wasn't very good in dealing with the public."[127]

In mid-September, polls had the candidates in a virtual dead heat with Branstad at 47 percent to Avenson's 44 percent. However, as the election neared, Branstad began to build a substantial lead. Two weeks before Election Day, a *Des Moines Register* poll showed the governor enjoying a nineteen-point lead over Avenson. By

November 1, 1990, Governor Branstad still dominated with a seventeen-point lead with 11 percent undecided.

On Election Day, November 6, 1990, Branstad crushed his opponent by a staggering margin of 21.8 points. He won ninety-six of the ninety-nine counties, taking all but Lee, Wapello, and Johnson. Of 976,483 votes cast for governor, Branstad had a total of 591,852 votes to Avenson's 379,372.

The downtown Des Moines Marriott hosted a third celebration for Governor Terry Branstad in his largest margin of victory for any of his elections. During his victory speech to his many supporters, Branstad said, "We have come a long way. We have only scratched the surface of what we can do with the state. I took over when times were tough, in the midst of the farm crisis, and we never gave up."

CHAPTER SEVEN

The Primary Gets Tough (The Election of 1994)

Early in his third term, in July 1991, Governor Branstad sent an earthquake-size rumble across Iowa when he announced a massive cutback in the public workforce. "Branstad fires 851 workers" roared one headline, with a sub-headline that said "Governor ponders laying off up to 1,100 more employees."[128]

The layoffs were projected to save about $20 million in operating costs per year, with the Department of Human Services losing 350 workers in one fell swoop. Union leaders immediately blasted the move, calling it a black day for the state. Shortly after, another 417 state employees were cut, and Branstad issued a long letter to Iowans, asking daily and weekly newspapers all across the state to print it. Here is what he wrote:

Last week I announced the completion of reduction in force in state government for this fiscal year. This action was necessary to balance the state's budget and begin to put our fiscal house in order. It was a difficult but necessary course of action to avoid a major state tax increase. My heart goes out to those people who are affected and I have initiated an outplacement program to assist them in their search for new jobs.

As governor of the state of Iowa, I have a duty to balance the interests of all Iowans, and I believe the majority of Iowans support the actions I have taken. The reduction in force is necessary because the state's expenditures cannot consistently exceed the taxpayer's ability to pay.

During the 117-day legislative session, I asked legislators to cut spending in order to balance the budget. The Legislature left without *balancing the budget, and that is why I cut $44 million through the item-veto process, saved another $100 million through a 3.25 percent across-the-board cut, and announced the reduction in force. I have also formed a statewide committee to recommend permanent reforms in state spending.*

With our state's population and personal income, state government is just too big and costly for what Iowans can afford. The only alternative to the item vetoes, the across-the-board cuts, and reduction in force was a major tax increase which would drive people, investments and private sector jobs out of our state. The hardworking people of Iowa must carefully match their own individual budgets to what they can afford; government must do the same. My goal is to build economic development so more Iowans can enjoy a better standard of living.

In 30 years, the size of state government has doubled while the population of the state is nearly the same. In 1960, the number of state employees for every 10,000 Iowans was 83; now that number is 167. Even more astounding is the fact that state and local government spending per capita has increased 810 percent, from $253 per person in 1960 to $2,303 per person in 1990.

State government salaries have grown much faster than Iowans' salaries in general in the past decade. The average weekly pay for state employees went from $278 in 1980 to $527 in 1990, in contrast to the $251 average weekly pay for all Iowans in 1960 and $366 in 1990. In the difficult decade of the 1980s, state employees received salary increases in nine of the past 10 years.

The percentage increase in the governor's salary over the past decade was only half that of the state employees. Contrary to what some have said, I did not receive a salary increase this year. In fact, because I have not requested the increases that other state employees received, there are now 1,057 state employees making more than the governor. There were only 27 in 1983 when I first took office.

I have taken firm action to fulfill my constitutional and statutory responsibility to balance the budget. The federal government and many other states are facing similar budget problems. By taking action now, I want to restore Iowa to a position of fiscal solvency and lead the rest of the nation in that direction. I am confident that I have acted in the best interest of the citizens of the state of Iowa, and I appreciate the many Iowans who have expressed support for these tough decisions.[129]

It was interesting to note that Branstad pointed out the salary increases for state workers as opposed to civilian workers. Also of note was the governor's salary. He stated that there were 1,057 state employees making more than the governor, while there were only twenty-seven when he first took office. Even though he never complained about the governor's salary, the desire to earn more money was one of the reasons that Branstad would point to when the time came that he was ready to leave office. "I promised my wife I'd try to make some money, so I'm doing that," he said four months after leaving office in 1999.[130]

There was more turmoil on the horizon. The 1994 Iowa gubernatorial election marked the first time a primary hopeful took on Governor Branstad. The challenger was Iowa's popular US congressman from the fifth district, Fred Grandy, and a spirited GOP primary campaign ensued.

Fredrick Lawrence "Fred" Grandy was born in Sioux City. He attended Phillips Exeter Academy in New Hampshire, where he was the roommate of President Dwight D. Eisenhower's grandson. Grandy received a bachelor's degree in English studies from Harvard University in 1970, earning magna cum laude honors. He considered attending law school but instead pursued a career in acting.

During the 1970s, Grandy landed spots on various national television shows. His best-known role was on the popular series *The Love Boat*, where he played the character Gopher from 1977 through 1986. After his acting days were over, Grandy ran for representative in the US Congress for the fifth district of northwest Iowa, serving four terms, from 1987 to 1995.

In December 1993, Grandy announced his candidacy to represent the Republican Party in the 1994 Iowa gubernatorial election. "I'm crazy enough to believe this party wants a choice," said Grandy. "I do not think this process is bad for the Republican Party, and I am firmly convinced it is good for the state of Iowa and essential to the work in progress we call democracy."[131]

He charged that Branstad had served too long in office, had failed to control the state budget, and had not built bipartisan consensus on key issues. While noting that the incumbent governor enjoyed strong support in the Republican Party across the state, Grandy said he thought Branstad was vulnerable to defeat during the general election.

The Democrats fielded three primary contestants for their nomination. Bonnie J. Pierce Campbell was the current Iowa Attorney General and wife of Ed Campbell, the Democrat gubernatorial candidate who lost in the primaries in 1982. A native of upstate New York, she was raised on a farm and later moved to Washington, DC. In 1969, she became a staff member for Iowa Senator Harold Hughes. She later moved to Iowa and oversaw the offices of Iowa Senator John Culver from 1974 to 1980.

Campbell graduated from Drake University in 1982 and earned her JD from Drake University Law School in 1985. From 1985 to 1991, she practiced law in Des Moines and served as the chair of Iowa's Democratic Party from 1987 until 1991. In the years 1990–1994, Campbell served as Iowa Attorney General, elected when the office was vacated by Tom Miller in his unsuccessful primary run for governor.

Campbell focused her campaign on state finances. She championed eliminating budget deficits, reexamining budget priorities, collecting money in fees and fines already owed to the state, eliminating tax code loopholes, and updating state technology.

Her opponent for the Democratic nomination for governor was Richard "Bill" Reichardt. Born and raised in Iowa City, he had a very successful high school athletic career and enrolled at the University of Iowa. In 1951, Reichardt earned all-America football honors as a fullback for the Hawkeyes and was voted the Big Ten's most valuable player. He earned a degree in economics. He played one season with the Green Bay Packers of the NFL, and during the Korean War he served in the US Air Force. Following his transition back to civilian life, Reichardt moved to Des Moines and started multiple businesses and organizations, including a popular men's formal wear store.

He represented Polk County for two years in the Iowa House of Representatives and was elected in 1966 to the Iowa State Senate, where he served four years. His platform focused on education. In particular, Reichardt wanted to bring thirty thousand dropouts back to school. He argued that "Eighty-five percent of adult prisoners were found guilty when they were juveniles. Ninety percent of people found in adult prisons dropped out of schools." Reichardt championed the idea that education was the key to grow the economy and reduce crime. He said the state's high tax rates should be restructured to attract new businesses and thwart individuals from moving away.

The third primary candidate, Darold Powers, campaigned on a bipartisan agreement for an economic package that included poorer counties in Iowa as benefactors for new economic development.

During the Republican primary, Grandy embarked upon a "Truth in Iowa" tour across the state, declaring that "Iowans deserve better." He said the top priority in his administration would be stimulating the economic development of the state through a proposed $500 million in state and property tax cuts, coinciding with a freeze on spending. He also championed the idea of the abolishment of parole for felons, a victim's bill of rights, and laws against gang members.

"This campaign is not negative but critical of the governor," he said. "He's not a bad guy. He's become a bad manager, but that's nothing that term limits can't cure." Grandy referred to Branstad as the "MasterCard Governor" and argued that the state was keeping "two sets of books" to hide deficits. "When the state keeps two sets of books, that's when it stops paying schools on time."[132] The "two sets of books" figure of speech stems from using different accounting methods to derive favored results.

In a column in the *Des Moines Register*, Dave Yepsen made the claim that the Branstad campaign's goal was to force Grandy out of the race before the primary by using strategies similar to what Bob Ray used successfully to force Roger Jepsen, Ray's lieutenant governor, from a bid to replace him on the ticket. Yepsen opined that the

Grandy campaign seemed to get a late start and was ineffectual at the outset. Yepsen cited the decision to use television ads so soon as a major snafu.

"Airing any kind of TV ads this early in the campaign baffled political operatives who say Grandy's following a Don Avenson media strategy—squandering resources on television ads long before most undecided voters were paying attention. Like Avenson's 1990 strategy, Grandy's early buys have the flavor of a desperate, go-for-broke Hail Mary football pass. The party poopahs smell a winner in Branstad. In politics, perception soon becomes reality where people want to go with a winner."[133]

Just twelve days later, in a column for the Associated Press, Mike Glover wrote that the two sides were clashing over style and tactics. "Branstad's tactic tends to confirm the thinking that he's seeking some kind of knockout punch to force Grandy from the race." Glover quoted Grandy as saying he was not going anywhere and that he was going to run a "radically different campaign than Terry Branstad. Iowa doesn't need two Terry Branstads, we already have one Terry Branstad too many."[134]

Meanwhile, Branstad's campaign was focused on continued economic growth, raising education standards, creating quality health care, and offering a tough crime program. He countered Grandy (and other critics) for the "two sets of books" allegations by referring to the expenditure limitation law that was created in 1992 that placed a 99.percent limit on expenditures. In addition, the law required the general assembly and the governor to use certain revenue estimates of the revenue estimating conference (REC). It also created the cash reserve fund, incorporated generally accepted accounting principles (GAAP) to standardize the state's accounting procedures, amended provisions of the economic emergency fund, and redirected the flow of the general fund surplus to fund the reserve funds and the GAAP deficit.

"I think I've made a big change," said the governor. "You think of what Iowa was like in January 1983 when I became governor, and then you look at it today, and what you see is a state with more focused quality education at our universities, economic development that created more quality jobs, and long-term agriculture research that is going to pay off down the road."[135]

He also told Glover that "a primary is an organizational battle. I think this is going to be a good test of our organization." Once again, his political instincts were about to be shown to be right on the mark.

Branstad picked up an important endorsement from fellow Republican and US Senator Charles Grassley. While touring northwest Iowa on his annual canvassing of all Iowa counties, Grassley threw his support behind Branstad.

"Representative Grandy has been an excellent congressman, and I don't doubt that he could be a good governor," said Grassley. "I normally don't get too involved with primary elections like this. But I chose to back Branstad because of several reasons. (Branstad) has dealt with a Democratic legislature since being elected. He has had to fight through droughts in 1983 and 1988, floods in 1993, agricultural disasters in 1985–1986. The (Iowa) economy has been really bad. I think he has done a pretty good job considering the situations he has faced. Branstad brings excellent leadership to the job as governor, and right now I don't think we should be changing leadership in the state of Iowa."

During that same session, Grassley also played the role of soothsayer and predicted the outcome of the primary with a Branstad win of a 52 to 48 percent margin of victory.[136]

On June 7, 1994, the scene was set. Voters created the largest turnout for an Iowa primary in forty-six years. By 10:00 p.m. that evening, with 25 percent of the precincts reporting, Branstad and Grandy were tied at 50 percent each. "It's going to be a long night," said a Grandy campaign worker at the Fort Des Moines Hotel. When the final results were tallied, a total of 311,277 voters had participated in the Republican primary. Governor Branstad had an edge of 161,228 to 149,809 votes over Grandy. Senator Grassley's prediction of a Branstad win with a 52 to 48 percent margin of victory had proved to be "spot on."

Hugh Winebrenner, a professor of public administration at Drake University, said, "The outcome was based more on personality and some political grudges than anything else." In his concession speech, Grandy said, "It's not my place to turn around now and say rally around the winner."[137] That statement, offering no symbolic conciliatory handshake, rankled many of Branstad's supporters and left an icy feeling in the air.

As for the Democratic primary, no drama occurred as Bonnie Campbell dominated the race with a stunning 78 percent to 19 percent win over Bill Reichardt. Darold Powers received only 2 percent of the vote.

Immediately following the primary, Governor Branstad started a "unity tour" in his Winnebago RV to rally and unify his party. Branstad offered an invitation to Grandy to join him, but the congressman declined. Bonnie Campbell immediately sought support from Grandy, but he didn't offer that, either.

The residue of the bitter GOP primary still lingered after two decades. "I think that campaign was very hard on the governor," said David Fisher in 2014. "There were some people that he thought were close to him that jumped on the Grandy bandwagon, and that hurt him. It really did. But he doesn't hold a grudge against anyone.

"I was at Terrace Hill the night of the election. About nine p.m. when the early returns came in, Grandy was ahead, and I thought it could be a tough night. But as the rural vote came in, the governor pulled ahead.

"I'm not sure, but I don't think he ever heard a word from Grandy, not even to this day," added Fisher.[138] That is indeed the case.

"At one point, Grandy's wife came up to Terry and said, 'Quit being so hard on Fred,'" said Lyle Simpson. "Actually, in our view, it was the other way around."[139] But what the Grandys found out about Terry Branstad, just as other opponents had discovered the hard way, was that he was a fierce competitor, a trait that he probably inherited from his mother.

"I was in 4-H Club and played baseball with him," said Riley Lewis, a farmer and businessman who was a grade behind Branstad in school and still lives in Forest City. "Rita had a strong voice and would sit right behind home plate. When she was after the umpire, it was 'Look out—Rita's on the warpath!' You could hear Rita all over the place when a call went against one of her sons. She would let the ump know what she thought. She was very nice, but also very competitive, for sure. You didn't mess with her boys," he added with a chuckle.[140]

For their part, the Democrats felt that the Republicans' tough primary struggle would work to their advantage. "They (the Iowa Republicans) have pushed themselves so far to the right that the Democrats will look like the party in the middle. That's right where we need to be," said Eric Tabor, chairman of Iowa's Democratic Party.[141]

The two candidates debated on October 5, 1994, in Des Moines, and both touted their agricultural roots to appeal to the masses. The highlight of the debate was Campbell's announcement of a new tax cut proposal totaling $230 million. Her plan was to repeal the one-cent tax increase that brought the sales tax to five percent, arguing that the savings would help all taxpayers, not just the wealthy.

As a rebuttal, Branstad stated that he deserved partial credit for her plan because his tax cut was offered first. "I'm really pleased to hear that my opponent has now admitted that we are in a position to reduce taxes. It wasn't easy to get there."

Branstad's tax deduction plan was to cut income taxes to create new jobs. He pointed out that the state sales tax was still under the national average while the income tax was the eleventh highest in the nation, driving retirees out of the state. Using his savvy debate skills, Branstad chided Campbell for bringing up the new plan so late in the race. "Up until tonight, she's said, 'No, I wouldn't promise any tax cut.'"

Campbell proposed to create or reinstitute government programs that included new science advisory panels for cutting-edge technologies, and spoke about reinstating the Iowa Crime Commission. Other topics included the economy, where Branstad highlighted his successful efforts for Iowa exports to foreign countries and three hundred thousand jobs created in the state. Branstad's reinstatement of the death penalty under certain circumstances versus Campbell's opposition to the death penalty was also a large topic.

Following the debate, Branstad's campaign took advantage of Campbell's newly minted tax cut plan announced at the debate to form a new bumper sticker slogan—"Don't Gamble on Campbell."

Governor Branstad kept his ticket intact from the previous election, and Joy Corning was again his running mate. On June 13, Campbell announced her running mate for lieutenant governor. The possibilities ranged from Iowa State Senate President Leonard Boswell of Davis City, State Senator Tom Vilsack of Mount Pleasant, State Representative Rick Dickinson of Sabula, State Democratic Chairman Eric Tabor of Baldwin, and John Chrystal of Coon Rapids. Her final choice was Boswell.

The general election was held on November 7, 1994, and 997,248 votes were cast for the office of governor. Branstad won by a landslide with 566,395 votes for 56.8 percent to Campbell's 414,453 votes for 41.6 percent. He also won ninety-four of the ninety-nine counties, including traditionally Democratic Polk County. The impressive 15 percent margin of victory would mark the beginning of a fourth term for the incumbent governor.

In her concession speech before a crowd of approximately two hundred supporters, Campbell said, "When you're on the track and the train is coming, folks, you're going to get mowed over. It always was my vision to give voice to the voiceless. I'll make my contribution in some other way, but I will never stop being an advocate for people who need it the most."[142]

A group of seven hundred Branstad supporters filled the Des Moines Marriott once again to celebrate. During his victory speech, Branstad expressed his gratitude for the large win and the dedicated voters.

"I am very humbled by the support and the strong vote of confidence that we've received tonight. We did it against the odds, against the anti-incumbent trend, against the pundits and against the stiffest competition we have ever seen. As governor, I am very honored and very proud to have this unique opportunity to serve a fourth and final term."[143]

The state was now poised to make history in the governor's office. And though few in the crowd that night realized it—including the governor himself, his family, and his closest advisers—the word "final" was not etched in stone.

"The Iowa Democratic Party establishment has long been perplexed with Branstad," wrote James Strohman in a cover story called "The Undefeated Governor" that ran in *CityView* on January 9, 2014, "at first salivating to run against him, then infuriated that he could be re-elected, and then mystified at how he could continue to stay in office for so many years."[144]

Strohman then expressed an opinion that sums up a good portion of the Leland native's astounding success: "The activists who control the party have consistently underestimated Branstad's political acumen and fail to understand his appeal with Iowa voters throughout the past four decades. They have enabled Branstad's success by nominating the wrong candidates to run against him, promoting campaign issues which are not popular with Iowans, and attacking the governor with critiques which have never resonated with voters."[145]

While all of that seems true enough, other factors have loomed large in the Branstad success story. They are well known among his closest advisers. First, there is his competitive nature, inherited from his mother. Then there are the tremendous organizational skills and the ability to study and listen to what others are saying. Finally, his passion for doing what he feels is best for the state and what the people of the state will respond to is exceptional.

"He reads everything that people send to him and puts in an incredible amount of time and effort to study the situation," said Lyle Simpson. "Every decision he makes is well thought out and is truly with the best interests of the state in mind. He really makes decisions unselfishly."[146]

"He's just so passionate, I've never met anyone so passionate," said his wife, Chris.[147]

Branstad's reputation was continuing to grow nationally as he was recognized not only for his strong election showings but as a politician who was well organized and got things done. In August 1996, he was the nation's senior state executive and was invited to address the national GOP convention in San Diego.

"In state after state, a new generation of Republican governors is reshaping the future and focusing on progress and opportunity," he said. "Thirty years of big government and federal solutions didn't work. Now, conservative Republican governors are changing government's mind-set, reawakening American federalism, and returning power to the states." He noted that at the time he was first elected there were just sixteen GOP governors and now there were thirty-two.[148]

On his fiftieth birthday, November 17, 1996, Branstad took time out from the world of politics to celebrate the occasion in a very nostalgic fashion. A 1950s-style dinner party was held at the Surf Ballroom in Clear Lake, the historic facility that rocked its way into music legendary status as the night the music died. Buddy Holly, the Big Bopper, and Richie Valens performed there on February 3, 1959, then were killed in a plane crash just west of the ballroom later that night.

"This is the year of Iowa's sesquicentennial, and I'm gonna admit that I'm turning fifty," he told Michele Applegate of the *Globe-Gazette* newspaper of Mason City. "As a kid growing up in the '50s, I used to come to the Surf . . . there's a lot of good memories of the Surf."[149]

While most insiders felt that Branstad would not run for a fifth term, there was still plenty of speculation that he just might decide to do so. One of the best of the editorial cartoons offered by the talented Brian Duffy of the *Des Moines Register* appeared on October 29, 1996. It showed a wide-eyed, frightened governor hiding under his desk while Chris Branstad stood over it on the other side, hands on hips, shouting, " Fifth term?! Where is he? Where is he?"

An interesting development was revealed several months later when David Yepsen wrote that Branstad was declaring he would not run again and suggested Senator Chuck Grassley consider taking his spot. Earlier, Senator Tom Harkin had hinted he might run for governor.

"I think Senator Grassley should be our candidate," said Branstad. "I think Grassley has a record that is in tune with Iowa. He's conservative and I think he can beat Tom Harkin and I think he stands for the values I believe in and I've encouraged Senator Grassley to run for governor."

". . . Branstad said he would enjoy a race against Harkin but that's not going to happen. 'My competitive side says, yes, but my practical side says, listen, I've made this commitment to my wife and to my family and from a financial perspective this is the time to go on and do something else.'"[150]

Neither Grassley nor Harkin took the bait and continued their long service as United States senators, Harkin retiring at the end of the 2014 term and Grassley still in office in 2015 in his sixth term.

In 1997, Branstad continued his involvement on the national scene. He chaired the prestigious Republican Governors Association, the Governors Ethanol Coalition, and the Education Commission of the States. In 1998, Branstad stressed his dedication to education once again by offering a huge plan that would eventually climb to unprecedented cost heights.

"The governor wants to make education the focus of the Legislature, and he has offered a package of reforms that include increase teacher pay, strengthen preschool programs, and all-day, every day kindergarten," reported the AP. "The governor included $19.2 million in his budget plan to finance his proposals in the first year. Annual cost of the effort eventually will surpass $100 million."[151]

Several months later, he even cancelled a trip to Russia to celebrate ten years of a sister-state relationship there. He opted to stay in Des Moines because he felt it was more important to get an education bill passed, and he was trying to convince lawmakers that a special session was needed.

"This is the most important issue facing our state," he said. "I'm convinced it can be done. We can't accept mediocrity. We've got to set our goal as being the best."[152]

Though he said he didn't want it passed piecemeal, that is precisely what happened.

By the end of his fourth term and after sixteen years in office, Branstad was looking forward to making large changes in his and Chris's lifestyle. He had given everything he had to offer to the state of Iowa, and he felt it was time to shift gears. They had made tremendous financial sacrifices, and both of them were concerned about their future, as serving as governor had not been nearly as financially successful as other positions could have been. In 1995, the governor's salary was just $76,700 per year, which was less than nearly 1,600 other state employees were making. By comparison, the head of the University of Iowa Hospitals was pulling in $290,700, and many others in high positions were earning well over $200,000. Hayden Fry, Iowa football coach, was paid $230,505, while Edward Stanek, commissioner of the Iowa Lottery, was at $91,359.

"Even some of the people Branstad has appointed to run state agencies make thousands of dollars more than the governor and other elected officials," wrote Jonathan Roos in the March 5, 1995, *Des Moines Register*. "It wasn't always that way. Seventeen years ago, only 27 state workers received more money than the governor. Since then, others' paychecks have grown at a faster rate than the governor's. . . .

"The governor's salary no doubt looks attractive to people who are paid less, especially since fringe benefits include the governor's mansion. But the really big salaries in state government these days are paid to university administrators, high-profile coaches, physicians and top professors."[153]

Jack Kibbie, a Democratic leader in the Iowa Senate who works on state budgets, told Roos, "It's odd that the governor is outnumbered by so many better-paid employees. If you were to have an executive that ran a company as large as state government, you'd probably have to put a couple of zeroes at the end of the governor's salary."[154]

During his years in office, Branstad's economic achievements were proof beyond doubt of his commitment to sound fiscal policy. Iowa's unemployment rate went from 8.5 percent when he took office to a record low 2.5 percent by the time he left office in 1999. In his first year as governor, the state budget had a $90 million deficit. It took several years until the budget was balanced, as he maintained he did not have enough support in the legislature to approve budget reforms until 1992.

When he decided not to run again, that left the door open for new candidates to show their stuff, on both sides of the aisle. Lt. Governor Corning tossed her hat in the ring but pulled out quickly. Former six-term US Congressman Jim Ross Lightfoot, a native of

Sioux City who was raised on a farm near Farragutc, became the Republican hopeful for the state's top position. At the outset, he seemed a good bet to continue the GOP dominance. But Tom Vilsack, a former mayor of Mount Pleasant and state senator, overcame long odds to defeat Lightfoot in a close 1998 election, becoming only the fifth Democrat to hold the office in the twentieth century.

On January 17, 1999, Branstad delivered his final "Condition of the State" address to the Iowa Legislature. "These past sixteen years have been the best years of my life," he said. "Thank you for giving this farm boy from Winnebago County the honor of being your governor." He added a thanks to "all of you who have put up with my moustache, my less-than-silver tongue, and my Iowa earnestness over these years." Following his speech and a standing ovation, the legislators passed an "extraordinary resolution" to honor his years of service to the state.[155]

Vilsack won again in 2002, over Doug Gross, an attorney who had earned his political stripes as an assistant to Robert Ray and chief of staff for Branstad. In 2006, after two terms as Iowa's fortieth governor, Vilsack launched a futile bid for the Democratic nomination for president and wound up as secretary of agriculture for President Barak Obama. Replacing Vilsack as governor was Chet Culver, former secretary of state. Born and raised in Washington, DC (his father was a US senator from Cedar Rapids), Culver graduated from Virginia Tech and returned to Iowa to earn a master's degree in education from Drake, embarking upon a teaching career. He taught government and history at Roosevelt High School and later Hoover before turning to politics.

Following efforts in field work for the Democratic Party of Iowa, Culver ran for secretary of state in 1998 and won, becoming at age thirty-six the youngest person holding that position in the entire nation at the time. He won reelection four years later and then decided to run for Vilsack's seat when the latter left to run for president.

Culver overcame a challenge by Jim Nussel, a native of Des Moines who served six terms in Congress, to win the 2006 election. Culver pounded out a 53–44 margin to become the state's forty-first governor and keep the Democrats in charge of the governor's office.

They also took control of both legislative branches for the first time since the mid-1960s. Unbeknownst to anyone at the time, Culver's victory also set the stage for the return of an Iowa icon.

Rita and Edward pose with their young son, Terry Edward, while the family is living on the farm in Leland.

Terry Branstad (right) and his young brother, Monroe, flash big grins for the camera.

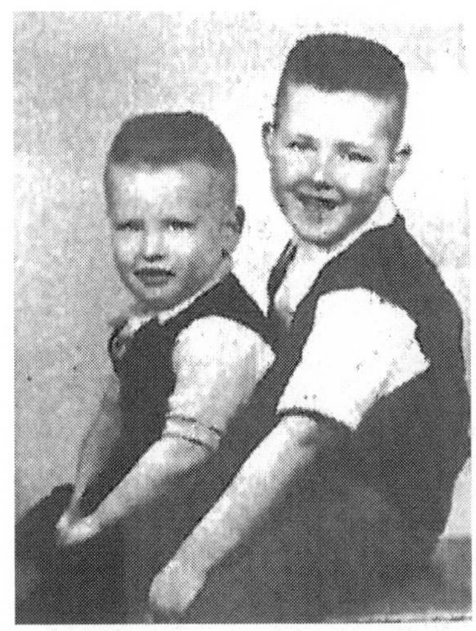

Monroe, also known as Monte, and Terry show off their new vest sweaters.

On this special occasion at church, the Branstads presented the image of the All-American family.

Terry Branstad's senior photo at Forest City High School in 1965 shows a determined young man ready to set off on a voyage that will take him to the University of Iowa, Drake Law School and to the top spot in Iowa government circles.

Terry was drafted into the Army (left photo) on September 17, 1969 and was assigned to the military police unit (right photo) in Fort Bragg, North Carolina.

Terry and Chris on their wedding day, June 17, 1972.

Lt. Governor serving with Governor Robert D. Ray.

Lt. Governor Terry Branstad addresses a fundraising crowd during his campaign for governor in 1982.

The Lt. Governor of Iowa and his young wife enjoy a moment at one of the many functions.

In 1982, Rita Branstad looks the proud mother as she and her son attend an evening event in Lake Mills, Iowa.

Edward and Rita made an effort to attend as many official events as possible during the time their son was governor.

Lura Sewick, the teacher who Governor Branstad attributes his interest in history. This photo was taken at Lura's 90th birthday party in Burt, Iowa.

In the early years at Terrace Hill, the Branstad family consisted of Terry and Chris, sons Eric and Marcus and daughter Allison.

Christmas at Terrace Hill was a big event for the family and for many Iowans who were given the opportunity to tour the mansion.

One of the highlights of Governor Branstad's career came when President Ronald Reagan visited Iowa on February 18, 1984. In the top photo, the President greets young Allison as the Governor and First Lady observe. In the bottom photo, the President poses with the Branstad family.

Ronald Reagan, 40th President of the United States and a former Des Moines radio broadcaster, is greeted by Governor Terry Branstad when the President came to Waterloo on February 18, 1984, for Caucus Night.

Governor Branstad received top advice from David Fisher, who served as his campaign advisor during the 1982 election cycle.

A number of county treasurers and legislators met in the Governor's Office for a monumental signing of the driver's license legislation. Connie Burton (Page Co. Treasurer), Chris Shelton (Fremont Co. Treasurer), Anita Walker (Montgomery Co. Treasurer), Sharon Winchell (Cass Co. Treasurer), Kim Reynolds (Clarke Co. Treasurer), Peggy Smally (Audubon Co. Treaserer), Nancy Boettger (State Senator), Jack Drake (Former House Rep.), JoAnn Johnson (Senator).

In the top photo: Governor Branstad with President XI Jinping April 29, 1985. Pictured left to right: Mr. Liu Luqing, Mr. Bai Runzhang, President XI jinping, Governor Terry Branstad, Mr. Xiqing Yu, Mr. Jiang Dehui and Ms. Jean Kaung (Iowa Sister States Board Member). Below, Chris and the Governor and President XI Jinping.

The Governor meets with two of his biggest supporters, Richard and Clara Johnson–who also happen to be his father-in-law and mother-in-law.

Lt. Governor Joy Corning occupies a special spot in Iowa history as she became a part of the first team to be elected as the state's top official from the same party. This election took place in 1990.

Members of the Branstad family occupied a special place at the 1991 Inaugural Ball. Sharing in the festivities were Edward (second from right) and his siblings (from left) Hubert, Helene and Carl.

Governor Branstad has always been a big supporter of veterans and their various activities. On this occasion, he visited the Veterans Memorial with a group of veterans.

Recognizing the stress of the job of directing the entire state's government, Terry Branstad placed a high premium on exercising, often taking brisk walks around Water Works Park with his good friend, Mel Straub.

A farewell for Governor Branstad during the last day in office for department head staff in 2000.

One of the activities that the governor enjoys the most involves volunteering in popular spots around the state - such as The Candy Kitchen in Wilton. The shop is a very local attraction in operation for over 100 years and is owned by Thelma and her late husband, Gus Nopulous.

RAGBRAI has become an institution in the state of Iowa, attracting thousands of riders for the annual trip across Iowa. The Governor and his young son, Eric, were among the riders in one of his early days as governor.

Gerald Weiner (right) and a guest (left) accompanied Governor Branstad on an important economic development trip to Russia.

The new 14th President of Des Moines University, former Governor Branstad, gives his Inaugural address to faculty, staff and family members in 2004. The University, at the time was celebrating its 106th year history. He served as president of the prestigious institution for six and a half years, resigning to run for governor once again.

The Branstad family celebrates the first Glanton Scholarship Dinner in 2004. President Branstad was instrumental in starting the scholarship to honor Judge Luther Glanton and his wife, Willie, with the scholarship presented to students who represented excellence and diversity.

The Governor and Chris received tremendous support from Uncle Ron Meyer, who was an educator in California for many years and always made it a priority to attend important events here in Iowa.

Governor Branstad and Kim Reynolds strike a victorious pose on the night of the election, November 10, 2011. The night was the culmination of the remarkable return to power by Iowa's longest serving governor.

Bill Knapp, one of Iowa's most influential real estate developers and a behind-the-scenes politician, poses with Governor Branstad and Lt. Governor Reynolds. For many years Knapp had been a Democratic supporter, but switched his allegiances to the GOP team for the 2014 election.

Bishop Richard Pates and Governor Branstad share a moment at a local event in Des Moines.

Two of the most popular Iowans ever – Governor Branstad and former Iowa Wrestling Coach Dan Gable – were the key figures in the Character Counts Awards Banquet held in Des Moines in 2013. Gable was that year's recipient. Also on hand were (from left) Jim Aipperspach, Randy Ediker, President of HyVee, and Scott Raecker, President of Character Counts.

Michael Reagan, son of former President Ronald Reagan, was the featured speaker at one Republican Party of Iowa yearly event. The former talk show host posed with the Iowa Governor after the event.

The Iowa State Historical Building was the site of a gala event on December, 2014, with legendary singer Simon Estes as the special guest. Attending the gala were (from left) Billie and Governor Ray, Simon Estes, Governor Branstad, Lt. Governor Reynolds and Mary Cownie, Director of Cultural Affairs for the State of Iowa.

On July 5th, 1997, the Governor and Chris were celebrating their 25th wedding anniversary. A close friend took him fishing for salmon and he caught this huge one-it took hours to get it in. Fortunately, they were able to have it packaged and brought home.

Photo of all of the formal delegation from Iowa to celebrate the Norman Borlaug statue being placed in Statuary Hall at the U.S. Capitol in honor of his 100th birthday. (From left to right) Congressman Loebsack, Former Congressman Braley, Congressman King, Former Congressman Latham, Senator Grassley, Senator Harkin, Congressman Boehner, Congresswoman Pelosi, Governor Branstad, Lt. Governor Reynolds, Secretary of Agriculture Vilsack and Ambassador Quinn.

Hunting was a big part of Governor Branstad's youth, and he often enjoyed the opportunity to go on hunting trips with friends, such as this 2013 outing in Texas. Joining the governor(second from the right) were Dr. Steven Leuth, President of Iowa State University(far right), Bruce Rastetter, current president of the Board of Regents (second from left)., Michael Gerdin and a local guide.

Governor Branstad participating with the Pony Express Group on a horseback ride. Each year he has chosen to be a part of the ride in honor of Camp Sunnyside.

The Governor was interviewed at the State Fair by Mark Pearson. They enjoyed doing their "farm talk" together.

Participating in the "Every Day" Tractor Ride in honor of Mark Pearson, whose voice was heard each day on the Farm Show at noon on WHO radio in Des Moines.

Terry E. Branstad, destined to become the longest serving governor in American history.

Governor Branstad has always been proud of his service days, shortly after graduating from the University of Iowa. In this 2014 photo, with the American Flag in the background, he displays a framed photo of himself as a military policeman in Ft. Bragg, North Carolina.

All cartoons used with permission from Brian Duffy.

HE KEEPS GOING, AND GOING...

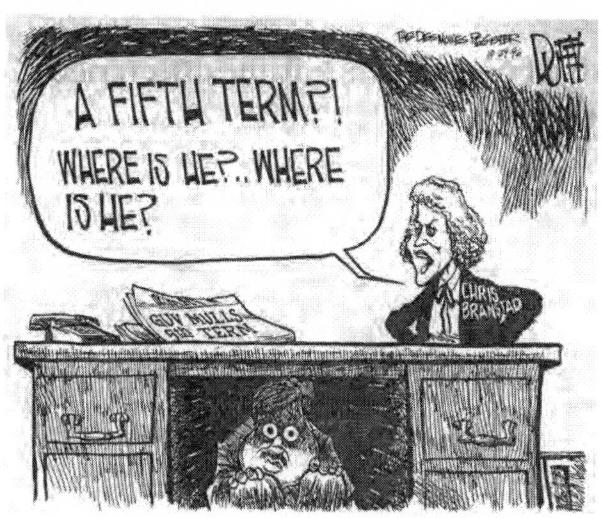
A FIFTH TERM?!
WHERE IS HE?.. WHERE IS HE?
CHRIS BRANSTAD
GOV MULLS 5TH TERM

ONE FOR THE THUMB...
1
2
3
4
duffyink.com

IHM GLD T BEH BAA
THEY CAN'T UNDERSTAND A WORD YOU'RE SAYING... I'LL INTERPRET FOR YOU.
PRESS CONFERENCE
MWA?
HE SAID HE'S CALLING FOR AN ACROSS-THE-BOARD TAX INCREASE...
UHN UH! UHN UH!
...A PAY RAISE FOR ALL LEGISLATORS...
GME FDR MDWR U @#*!
...HE WILL NOT BE RUNNING FOR RE-ELECTION AND WILL ENDORSE A DEMOCRAT FOR YOUR NEXT GOVERNOR.
DUFFY

I BELIEVE IN STAYING IN SHAPE.
EVERY DAY I HEAD OUT FROM MY OFFICE AT DES MOINES UNIVERSITY FOR A BRISK WALK DOWN GRAND AVENUE.
LATELY I'VE BEEN THINKING ABOUT ADDING SOME HILLS TO MY WORKOUT.
TERRACE HILL
DUFFY

CHAPTER EIGHT

Life after Terrace Hill

Following his departure from the governor's office on January 15, 1999, Branstad waded through a stack of offers, trying to figure out where he'd feel most comfortable. He soon entered into private business and formed Branstad and Associates LLC, and also became a partner in the firm of Kauffman, Pattee, Branstad and Miller. He did some consulting and even taught a class in public sector management at the University of Iowa, alternating between the Pappajohn Business Administration Building in Iowa City and the College of Business Administration's campus in Newton.

"We are pleased that Governor Branstad is coming to the University of Iowa," said Mary Sue Coleman, U of I president. "As a nationally-recognized leader in state government, he will bring a wealth of experience to our students, sharing his knowledge one-on-one in the classroom."[156]

In March 1999, it was announced that Branstad would head up the campaign of Lamar Alexander for the Republican presidential nomination. The former governor of Tennessee said he was trying to improve upon his third-place finish in the 1996 Iowa caucus by adding two proven winners—a focus on education and the high approval rating of the former governor.

Branstad also wanted to get into the field of financial planning and passed the series 7 security exam. He became a financial adviser with the Robert W. Baird Company in West Des Moines for three years. President George W. Bush appointed him to chair the President's Commission for Excellence in Special Education, with the goal of developing plans to improve the performances of students with disabilities. He also kept busy by serving on several commissions and boards. But everything shifted to a higher playing field in August 2003 when he was chosen for the position of president of Des Moines University.

There are several institutions in the Des Moines metro area offering higher education—Drake University, Grand View University, American Institute of Business—while Des Moines University and Mercy College of Health offer graduate-level degrees in medicine and health-related fields. Simpson College, Upper Iowa University, and William Penn University all have classroom facilities there. DMACC (Des Moines Area Community College) has six campus locations around the state, including those in Des Moines, West Des Moines, and Ankeny.

Although not well known even in Iowa, Des Moines University has a long and distinguished record in its field. It is the second-oldest osteopathic medical college in the nation, having been established in 1898. It is also currently the fifteenth-largest medical school in the United States, with some 1,662 enrolled students in 2014 and a faculty of forty instructors.

It was first called the Dr. S. S. Still College of Infirmary and Osteopathy & Surgery after its founders, Summerfield Saunders Still and his wife, Dr. Ella Still, who had come from Missouri. In 1905 the name was shortened to just Still College. In the 1940s, it was called Des Moines Still College of Osteopathy and Surgery. It went through several more name changes before its current name was adopted in 1999.

The college occupies twenty-two acres of the former St. Joseph's Academy facility at 3200 Grand Avenue and offers its students a very attractive and updated campus. The institution broadened its base in 1980 when the board of trustees voted to establish the College of Podiatric Medicine and Surgery and the College of Biological Sciences (now the College of Health Sciences). Despite its lofty reputation in the medical world, it was not well known in Iowa. When President Dr. Richard M. Ryan Jr. retired in 2002, the board of trustees was interested in finding a skilled leader who could enhance its status and name recognition.

Even though he had served on the board and had been a four-term governor of the state, Branstad was not an automatic choice. He had to go through an extensive interview process just like any other candidate. "In fact, he almost didn't get the job," said Doug Gross. "Several of us worked very hard to help get him, though, and in the end he was accepted by just one vote. Apparently some of the board members didn't think he had what it would take to relate to professors and doctors."[157]

But like many political "experts," they underestimated Branstad's resolve and his innate ability to charm people and win them over. On August 15, 2003, he became the fourteenth president of the highly respected medical university. He immediately went to work with the same energy and enthusiasm that he had taken into the governor's office, intent upon raising the visibility and prestige of the college. He also developed an outreach program for students.

"Once a month, students would sign up to have lunch with me, and I would ask them what they liked and did not like about Des Moines University," said Branstad in 2014. "I enjoyed the discussions, and it was helpful."[158]

One of the student ideas was to have all the classrooms wired for Internet use. "We got that done, and it really helped me with students," Branstad said. He also worked to expand enrollment, which he accomplished. Under his leadership, the endowment expanded from $50 million to $89 million, and he initiated improvements to the facilities. A new wellness center was added during his time at Des Moines University, and he still uses it today, as he lives at Terrace Hill just nine blocks east of the campus.

On the personal side, the governor's children had grown up in Terrace Hill, and moving out was not an easy task. Alison and Eric were gone to college, but Marcus was nearly fifteen and still living at home after two years in Leland on the farm. After sixteen years in Terrace Hill, the Branstads bought a house on the south side of Des Moines but continued searching for their ideal home.

"We had always wanted to have a log home, and we did a lot of research over the next three years," said Chris Branstad. "I can't tell you how many miles we drove, looking for the right place. One day,

Terry's barber, Al Thompson, arranged for us to look at a place about forty-five miles from Des Moines. We just loved the setting."[159]

The log house they bought was located on seventeen acres in Boone County, and the Branstads lived there for nine years. It may have seemed as if they were ready to settle in for the long run, but that wasn't the case. While Iowa had done fairly well on a fiscal basis during Vilsack's eight-year tenure, the state fell into huge financial debt during the Culver term. Also, Culver was criticized by some for a brusque manner of governing, and there was a general sense of unhappiness among Iowans all across the state. Among those who were frustrated enough to do something was Terry Branstad. He began to ponder the possibility of running again for governor . . . a decision that would dramatically alter his way of life, surprise many close friends, force a showdown with his wife, and catapult him into the national record books.

CHAPTER NINE

The Comeback
(The Election of 2010)

"After leaving the governor's office in January of 1999, Terry Branstad found his niche as Des Moines University's president," wrote Craig Robinson in the June 26, 2010 issue of the *Iowa Republican* magazine. "The role fit him well and the school flourished under his leadership."[160]

Robinson was correct on both accounts. But something was missing in Branstad's life. Maybe it was the thrill of competition that he had thrived on all his life, or maybe it was the sense of impending fiscal disaster for the state he loved so dearly and wanted to see basking in economic prosperity.

On Tuesday, January 19, 2010, Terry Branstad once again officially announced his candidacy for his previous office of governor after an eleven-year hiatus. In opening remarks to enthusiastic applause at the State Historical Society Building, Branstad began, "I'd like to start today with one simple question—Are you ready for a comeback?" The audience's response was totally supportive, of course, but it wasn't an easy or smooth decision for anyone closely connected to the Branstad family. Chris wasn't overjoyed. "It was tough, very tough," she said candidly. "There was some screaming. I thought he'd done it for sixteen years and that he'd done enough. But then I thought it over and felt I can't stand in his way. It means so much to him."[161]

Several of his closest friends admit they were caught off guard when Branstad talked to them about the possibility of returning to public office.

"I was not surprised when he was first elected governor," said Richard Schwarm in 2014, speaking from his law office in Lake

Mills, "but I admit I was surprised when he decided to come back. He had a great job at Des Moines University . . . terrific salary, security, retirement plan, and benefits. It seemed like a great situation for him."[162]

Schwarm had previously served as chairman of the Republican Party of Iowa and in 2009 was part of a group that searched high and low for a candidate to oppose Culver.

"We had people who were capable, but they weren't willing to jump in and make the sacrifices necessary. Terry was helping us look for a good candidate," said Schwarm. "One day he said, 'This may sound like a long shot, but how about me?'

"Lots of people close to him were kind of discouraging him at that point. We said, 'You've done your time, you've done enough. You don't need to do it again.'"[163]

Doug Gross, his chief of staff from 1984 to 1989, was on the same side as Schwarm, trying to talk his former boss and longtime friend out of coming back. Gross had made a run for governor himself in 2002, losing by eight points to incumbent Tom Vilsack. He fully understood the challenges and the sacrifices that awaited Terry Branstad should he decide to fight his way back into the seat of power.

"I was on the Iowa First Committee, a group that we had formed to see if we could find someone to run for governor in 2010," said Gross, sitting in his office at the law firm of Brown, Winick in the Ruan Building in downtown Des Moines. "Terry was on the committee too. We profiled the kind of person we'd like to see as governor.

"He called me one day and said, 'We're not having any luck finding that person . . . and we keep looking for a person like me. Well, I think I'd like to run again. What do you think?'"[164]

Gross thought it was a mistake and told him so, using basically the same arguments that Chris, Schwarm, and others had used—that he had served his time and needed to think of his own financial future. But Terry kept saying he wanted to run and have a chance to turn the economy back to the prosperity it had known under its Republican governors. When he left office in 1999, the state had a $900 million surplus. In 2010, the state was facing a projected $900 million deficit.

"Branstad's name never entered into the 2010 gubernatorial campaign discussion until May of that year," reported Craig Robinson. "By that time, some candidates had been in the race for over four months, and the field of potential candidates was about to explode to seven. The field shrank as quickly as it expanded once news of Branstad's return occupied the political columns in every newspaper for months."[165]

Terry was undeterred by the resistance he was encountering from those who mattered most. He had made up his mind to walk away from a very secure and lucrative job, with more than twice the salary he could draw as governor. Once he had his wife's blessing, the door was open for a shot at the job he truly loved. On October 16, 2009, he announced that he was leaving his position as president of Des Moines University after six successful years to seek the governorship once again.

Immediately following the historic declaration, Jeff Boeyink was introduced as the man who would head up the campaign. It was a job for which Boeyink was ideally suited. A graduate of Central College in Pella with a master's degree in public administration from Iowa State University, he was a former executive director of the Republican Party of Iowa and was widely respected for his managerial skills.

"I was three weeks too young to vote for Ronald Reagan in 1980," said Boeyink in 2014, sitting in his office at the LS2group in Des Moines. "Terry Branstad was the first person I ever voted for, back in 1982. And I had worked with him when I was a lobbyist in the 1990s. So, here I was in 2010, coming to work for him.

"Actually, this was the first campaign where Terry was able to spend full time working on it. In previous campaigns, he had a full-time job, but this time around he had retired from Des Moines University; it was a new experience for him. You may have heard about the Terry Branstad work ethic, but it's hard to believe until you see the man in action. He was on the phone day after day, working, working.

"We had a two-month window to raise $1.5 million. The governor would help us open envelopes, and he would get just as excited about a little check from someone at a large donation. It was an amazing experience for everyone."[166]

Branstad's "Iowa Comeback Tour" began in Des Moines and continued to seventeen cities in four days. The former governor campaigned on bringing back to Iowa ". . . the greatness we know we have in us." He touted his successful sixteen years of prior service as governor and shared his vision for the future by using the same blueprint he had always used. "How are we going to do it?" asked Branstad. "The way we have always done it. Setting ambitious goals. And we won't stop working until we get them done."

Branstad championed balancing the budget and restoring fiscal discipline as his highest priority when returning as chief executive of the state. "When we get that done, the rest of our dreams and goals are possible," he said. However, to win back the office of governor, Branstad would first have to face two other challengers for the Republican nomination.

Bob Vander Plaats was born and raised in Sheldon. After high school, Vander Plaats attended Northwestern College in Orange City and received a bachelor's degree in education and eventually his master's degree at Drake University. He taught at Boone and Jefferson and then became the principal at Marcus-Meriden-Cleghorn High School and Sheldon High School. He eventually went into both business and politics. In 2002, living in Sioux City, Vander Plaats ran unsuccessfully for the Republican gubernatorial nomination, losing to Doug Gross.

In 2006, Vander Plaats again ran for the same office but bowed out of the race to become Jim Nussel's choice for lieutenant governor. A staunch social conservative, Vander Plaats's base was Iowa's evangelical conservatives, and he was subsequently endorsed by former Arkansas Governor and presidential hopeful Mike Huckabee, the Iowa Family Policy Center, and James Dobson, the founder of Focus on the Family.

The other Republican vying for the party nomination was Iowa State Representative Rod Roberts from Carroll. Born in Waverly, Roberts graduated from NESCO Community High School and received his bachelor's degree from Iowa Christian College in Des

Moines. During the primary campaigning, Roberts touted his ten-year experience in the state legislature and the fact that he stayed "above the fray" and refrained from attacking his opponents.

Branstad's campaign in the primary was twofold. First, he showed his vision of the future, in part by demonstrating his successes from the past. No other candidate had the ability to substantiate their positions as well as Branstad because of his long record of accomplishment. Secondly, he never took his eye off the general election and continually pointed out the differences and shortfalls of the Culver administration.

"Branstad has run his campaign the same way that has led him to eleven straight victories," wrote Craig Robinson. "He is pro-life and supports an amendment to the state constitution to define traditional marriage. However, Branstad has been careful not to make his campaign about those issues. While he is asked about those issues and speaks to them at most of his campaign stops, the focus of his campaign is on pocketbook issues and jobs."[167]

The three primary candidates held three debates, and a routine could be seen throughout: Branstad was focused on his vision, qualifications, and the Culver administration. Vander Plaats attacked Branstad and challenged his record and credibility, leading the former governor to defend himself. Vander Plaats chose to use the same tactics as Fred Grandy in the 1994 gubernatorial primary, insisting that as governor Branstad had used "two sets of books" to hide deficits. As before, Branstad refuted the claims and referenced the expenditure limitation law from 1992 and moving the state to the standardized generally accepted accounting principles method of accounting. Roberts didn't attack either candidate, but his exposure was overshadowed by the fireworks created by Vander Plaats.

On June 5, 2010, the *Des Moines Register* Iowa poll showed Branstad having a 57 to 29 percent lead over Vander Plaats, with Roberts polling 8 percent. Branstad also had a commanding lead of 70 percent as best able to beat Governor Culver in the general election. According to the poll, the majorities of born-again Christians, supporters of the tea party movement, and first-time Republican primary voters backed Branstad to be the GOP nominee for governor.

The 2010 primary was held on June 8, 2010, and 229,731 votes were cast to decide the GOP nominee. Of those, Branstad commanded 111,450 votes, or 50 percent. Vander Plaats garnered 93,058 votes, or 40 percent, and Rod Roberts ended with 8 percent. Ultimately, the GOP voters chose a nominee who was focused more on economic issues than hot-button social issues.

"Iowa Republicans have decided that our state is ready for a comeback," Branstad said in his victory speech to supporters at Seven Flags Events Center in Clive. "We are united because we're all here for one reason, to give Iowans a government that is as good as the people of this state; a government that spends less, taxes less, interferes less, and indebts us less; a government that helps create more jobs, more well-schooled Iowans, more strong families, and more thriving small businesses in all parts of our state.

"And I, as your candidate for governor, give you my solemn commitment to be a governor as good as our people. Just as hard-working, just as frugal, just as honest. And just as committed to our values.

"To those businesses struggling to make the next payroll, to the workers hunting for good work for good jobs, for those communities fighting to stay alive, to those families hoping for a better education for their kids, I say change is coming.

"For those Iowans who want open, honest, and scandal-free government, change is coming.

"For those Iowans who want a government as good as they are, change is coming.

"And I'm proud to lead that change. We did it before, and we can do it again."

Incumbent Iowa Governor Culver was unchallenged in the Democratic primary and netted 56,293 votes. Once the primary was finished, the general election campaigning got under way quickly, showcasing the stark differences between the former and current governors. Branstad attacked Culver's spending—in particular, Culver's signature program, Iowa's Infrastructure Investment Initiative, or I-JOBS program, which included a $1.265 billion borrowing plan, according to the state treasurer's office. The program was similar to previous Democratic gubernatorial candidate programs, including those of Roxanne Conlin in 1982 and Lowell Junkins in 1986, in that it created government programs that would saddle the state with substantial long-term debt. Branstad said the problem with I-JOBS was that it diverted money used to finance the state's Rebuild Iowa Infrastructure fund, which controls construction of state buildings and other infrastructure projects.

"The fact is those receipts would have gone to good projects all around the state," he charged. "Instead, we are going to be paying back that debt. I believe in doing things on a pay-as-you-go basis."[168]

Branstad touted his successful navigation through the farm crisis and the reduction of large debts to a $900 million reserve when he left office in 1999. He also reminded voters that during his tenure, high unemployment had dropped considerably. The current unemployment rate (in 2010) was at 6.8 percent.

"If you look at the totality of my record, you'll see that we not only made Iowa more competitive, we took Iowa from being one of the high-tax states to below average in terms of taxes. I took Iowa from 8.5 percent unemployment to 2.5 percent unemployment."[169]

In Sioux City on September 14, 2010, at the end of their first of three debates, Governor Culver brought up the hot-button social issues, such as abortion rights and same-sex marriage.

"He's against women's rights. He's against civil rights. He's against an independent judiciary," said Culver. As he spoke, former Governor Branstad chuckled. In a *Des Moines Register* interview after the debate, Branstad replied, "I'm about as extreme as vanilla ice cream. Iowans know me. They know I've been a common-sense conservative."[170] The Democratic Governors Association the week prior released a memo noting the organization was advocating a strategy of painting Republicans as extremists.

For the second position on the ballot, Branstad mentioned during the campaigning and in the primary debates that if he won the nomination, he would find a lieutenant governor who would share his economic and social conservatism. He found those attributes in Iowa State Senator Kim Reynolds, from Osceola. Steve Roberts, a GOP activist and former national committeeman from

Des Moines, called Reynolds an excellent choice for lieutenant governor. "She brings a lot to the table," Roberts said. "She's been a local official, she's had experience running both at the local level and running for the legislature and yet she isn't considered part of the establishment."[171]

"It was an unbelievable honor of a lifetime," said Reynolds in 2015. "I received a call to come in and interview with his staff. As a prior country treasurer and newly elected state senator from a small town in south central Iowa, it wasn't a call I expected. Then I received a second call and I thought, 'This is serious!'"

She and her husband, Kevin, went to dinner with Terry and Chris Branstad and had, Reynolds said, a wonderful time. Branstad told her he was interested in building a team that would work closely together. "I really admired and respected his perspective that the lieutenant governor should be active in all aspects," she added.[172]

After being selected, Reynolds said it was a little surreal; she was excited to get started and proud to be a part of Branstad's team. "I had been appointed to the IPERS board and worked with him on driver's license issues, but I hadn't had much interaction with the governor prior to being selected. I've now seen firsthand how open-minded he is . . . how very thoughtful, deliberate, courageous, and what a great listener he is, and how hard he works on behalf of Iowans. He is truly a champion for Iowans at every level."[173]

For his part, Governor Culver retained his running mate from the 2006 ticket, Patty Judge.

The day before the general election, both candidates were on the campaign trail. Culver traveled by train on a whistle-stop tour of central and eastern Iowa, and although trailing in the polls, he tried to be optimistic. "We can just nick them at the finish line," he was quoted by *The Gazette* of Cedar Rapids on November 1.

While in eastern Iowa, Branstad fired back. "I know he (Culver) likes to campaign, but he hasn't governed. People want a governor that is going to be hands-on, going to meet with people, going to listen to people and put together an agenda that is going to work for Iowa."[174]

On Election Day, Tuesday, November 2, 2010, history was in the making. Of the 1,133,430 votes cast, the Branstad/Reynolds ticket received 592,494 votes for 52 percent of the vote. The Culver/Judge ticket tallied 484,798 votes for 42 percent. For the first time since 1962, when Norman Erbe lost to Harold Hughes, an incumbent governor of Iowa was ousted from the office.

During his concession speech at the Hotel Fort Des Moines, Governor Culver thanked his family, staff, and supporters. He mentioned how proud he was of his administration, noting it had raised the minimum wage, overturned Iowa's ban on stem cell research, and raised teachers' pay in Iowa to the national average.

At his victory speech at the Hy-Vee Conference Center in West Des Moines, Branstad said to his raucous supporters, "I'm more excited about the job ahead than I was the very first time I stood before you on an election night. You see, it is a privilege to serve Iowans." His victory made him Iowa's first five-term governor and also secured his spot in the national record book.

According to the website Smart Politics, Branstad actually moved into the no. 1 spot in American history in his second week in office in 2011 when he hit the 5,852-day mark to pass Bill Janklow of South Dakota by one day. Janklow rolled up his impressive run during two separate stints, from 1979 to 1987 and again from 1995 to 2003, for a total of sixteen years and seven days.

But some sources have also given credit to New York's George Clinton for being the longest serving governor, way back in the 1770s. The discussion centers on the fact that Clinton first took office several years before New York became a state, and Smart Politics doesn't acknowledge the pre-Constitution portion of his service as an official record. The brigadier general assumed the role on July 9, 1777, and served until 1795, and then again from 1801 to 1804. He was in that office for twenty-one years, but Smart Politics only recognizes those who served their entire time in the post-U.S. Constitution period. After Branstad's last election, here is how the Des Moines Register framed the situation in an article on November 4, 2014:

"With his win tonight, he'll be in a position to overtake George Clinton, the founding father who served as governor of New York both before and after the United States won independence from

Britain. Clinton served 7,641 days in office. To get to 7,642, Branstad must serve until December 14, 2015..."

That is also the date that Governor Branstad looks to, as well... removing all doubt.

When his fifth term expired on January 9, 2015, Branstad had been in office for an incredible 7,303 days over nineteen years, eleven months, and twenty-nine days. That is 24.5 percent longer than any other governor in history, according to Smart Politics.[175]

Janklow stands in second place on the list, followed by Alabama's George Wallace, with 5,848 days over sixteen years and four days. Wallace first took office in 1963 and last held the seat in 1987, but was out of office twice during that span. Jim Rhodes of Ohio is fourth on the list.

Often overlooked is the fact that Robert Ray holds the fourteenth spot, having served as governor for thirteen years, eleven months, and thirty days, for a grand total of 5,112 days.[176]

The 2010 victory also gave Branstad an amazing record of 18–0 in all elections up to that point. But there was even more to come. On January 15, 2014, to the surprise of absolutely no one, he announced that he would run one more time—going for a sixth term and a place in the history books that may never be matched. He was flush with enthusiasm from a successful three years of his fifth term and seemed a shoo-in for yet another milestone achievement.

"Gov. Branstad is as popular now as he's been since his return to office in 2010, with a 58 percent approval rating in the new Iowa Poll," wrote Kathie Obradovich in the June 8, 2013, *Des Moines Register*. "He's perhaps as well liked as he'll ever be until he finally leaves office or dies, whichever comes first. He's enjoying a host of favorable conditions that would seem to make his choice a no-brainer."[177]

Surrounded by his family and Lieutenant Governor Kim Reynolds's family and supporters, Branstad took center stage once again to make his announcement to a crowd of 250 at the Hy-Vee Conference Center in West Des Moines. "Four years ago, I saw the future of our state getting bleaker. I love this state. I was sick of the direction we were going. I knew we could do better, and four years ago, I came back to lead the Iowa comeback. And we've done it. My commitment to job creation and opportunities for Iowa's families drives me to say tonight that I intend to seek reelection as governor of this great state."

"The governor's race now officially pits incumbent Republican Terry Branstad against likely Democratic nominee Jack Hatch," wrote Jennifer Jacobs the next morning in the *Des Moines Register.* "It pits the comfy blanket Iowans have known for decades against a political street fighter with progressive ideas he says will improve the state."[178]

Two months later, Obradovich wrote that she had run into a gentleman at church who said he thought Branstad was doing a pretty good job but wasn't going to vote for him because he felt he had been in office long enough and it was time for a new face.

She responded thusly: ". . . Branstad has one of the highest job approval ratings of his current term, over $4 million in the bank at the end of last year, and a 15-point lead over his likely challenger. I think my church friend is going to need divine intervention if he wants to avoid another four years of Terry Branstad."[179]

The incumbent governor did have an opponent for the Republican nomination. Tom Hoefling from Lohrville, a tiny town in Calhoun County in west central Iowa, ran on a conservative platform that he said offered a " . . . principled, practical, concise alternative to the party platform of recent years." Hoefling is founder of American's Party and ran for president in 2012 under the American Independent Party. He criticized the growth of the state budget during Branstad's fifth term and faulted him for not acting more decisively in opposition to abortion and same-sex marriage. On June 3, 2014, Governor Branstad easily won the primary with 83.2 percent to Hoefling's 16.8 percent.

A real estate developer from Des Moines, Hatch was unopposed in the primary, as apparently no other Democrat saw any upside to facing Branstad this time around. Hatch served in the Iowa House of Representatives from 1985 to 1993 and in 1993 accepted the position of state director under US Senator Tom Harkin. Upon leaving that position, he returned to the Iowa House after winning election in November 2000. In 2002, Hatch was elected to the Iowa Senate, where he served as he pursued the gubernatorial office in 2014.

Branstad accepted invitations to three debates—on August 14 at the Iowa State Fair, September 20 in Burlington, and October 14 in Sioux City. During interviews, Hatch and his campaign repeatedly noted the governor's many experiences debating opponents while in office while minimizing his own past debates campaigning for and during his tenure in the Iowa legislature. "It's really a much different environment that I'm preparing for," Hatch said. "There's not much chance for the governor or me to exchange comments to each other."[180]

During the three debates, Hatch was unable to destabilize the momentum of the incumbent governor and his campaign. "Everything is really going in the direction of Gov. Branstad at this point . . ." said Christopher Larimer, a University of Northern Iowa political scientist, in mid-August. "The difficulty for Hatch is that he still needs to make the case that there's a systemic problem with the Branstad administration. I'm not sure he's going to be able to do that with two and a half months left."[181]

Just days before the election, the *Des Moines Register* Iowa poll had Branstad leading by a commanding twenty-four points over his challenger. On Election Day, the results were indeed fitting for the man who already held the title of the longest serving governor in Iowa history and, with a victory, was positioned to officially become the longest serving governor in American history, no strings attached.

Branstad swept ninety-eight of the ninety-nine counties in the state of Iowa. The only county that did not fall in his column was the Democratic bastion of Johnston County, home of the University of Iowa in Iowa City. In total, the governor garnered fifty-nine percent of the vote with a winning margin of 22.7 percentage points, tying his largest gubernatorial victory in his six elections. The victory was so decisive the race was called almost immediately after polls closed. Branstad had 666,023 votes to 420,778 for Hatch, while Lee Heib had 20,319 for the Libertarian Party. Two others in the race were Jim Hennanger (10,592 votes) and Jonathon Narcisse (10,239 votes).

It was part of a huge Republican wave all across the state, and much of the credit was given to the Branstad machine reaching out to help his party in other races. Joni Ernst, a state senator from Red

Oak, polled 52 percent of the vote to defeat early front-runner Bruce Braley, a four-term US congressman from Waterloo, and became the first female in Iowa history to go to the United States Senate. Her long, bruising battle was Iowa's most expensive race ever , with a total of $79 million spent. Branstad had personally supported her for months and predicted in early 2014 that she would be the party nominee and defeat Braley.

Additionally, Republicans David Young took the third district race and Rod Blum the first, while Steve King breezed to his seventh term in the fourth district. The second district stayed in the hands of Dave Loebsack, a Democrat. Republicans also gained control of more House seats in the state legislature, but the senate remained in Democratic control by a 26–24 margin.

In his acceptance speech at the West Des Moines Marriott Hotel, Branstad declared, "Four years ago, I returned to lead Iowa's comeback. Ladies and gentlemen, we've done just that. We've laid the foundation to make Iowa the envy of the nation, and I'm proud to say we're well on our way, but we're not done yet."

That could be an understatement of classic proportions. In his final years at the helm, the politician from the farm near Leland will leave a mark on the history books that may never be matched in Iowa.

CHAPTER TEN

The Chinese Connection

In 1972, President Richard Nixon visited the People's Republic of China, thereby initiating an important step to formally normalize relations between the two countries. When Air Force One touched down on February 21 in Beijing, it marked the first time a US president had visited the China mainland, and officially ended over two decades of isolation between the nations. The meeting is now considered by most scholars to be one of the most meaningful events in recent US history.

"This was the week that changed the world," said Nixon while visiting Shanghai. He stressed that what was most important was "what we will do in the years ahead to build a bridge across 16,000 miles and 22 years of hostilities which have divided us in the past. And what we have said today is that we shall build that bridge."[182]

No American governor has taken Nixon's message more to heart than Terry Branstad. Some eleven years later, on July 22, 1983, Governor Branstad signed a formal agreement with then Governor Zhang Shuguang of Hebei Province in China that established the sister-state relationship between Iowa and the province. Branstad noted during the signing that it was a diplomatic milestone for the state of Iowa. The sister-state relationship provided an opportunity for Governor Branstad and a fifty-person delegation to visit Hebei Province in 1984. A Chinese delegation reciprocated the exchange the next year, cosponsored by the Iowa Sister-State Friendship Committee and the Chinese People's Association for Friendship with Foreign Countries.

On April 24, 1985, a five-member delegation from Hebei Province of the People's Republic of China arrived in Iowa for an agricultural research trip, following the successful Iowa visit the year prior. The delegation sought ideas to help the agriculture-rich region of northern China. Among the Chinese local party officials was Xi Jinping, a rising political figure and a man destined to become president and general secretary of the largest nation on earth. Xi Jinping and his delegation met with Governor Branstad in the governor's office on April 29, 1985.

The delegates were hosted by a group of Iowans and accompanied by Lucca Berrone, the marketing manager of international trade for the Iowa Development Commission. The delegation initially spent time in Des Moines and Cedar Rapids and then stayed in Muscatine for two days, touring local farms and businesses. The delegation even received the key to the city from the Muscatine mayor.

Governor Branstad asked Sarah Lande, leader of the sister-states committee, to organize the Muscatine event. Lande and her hosts were constrained by a limited budget, so they relied on good, old-fashioned Iowa hospitality and home-cooked meals instead of bookings at elaborate hotels and restaurants. Xi spent two nights with the Eleanor and Thomas Dvorchak family a few blocks from the Lande home. There, Xi slept in their son's bedroom, decorated with a Star Trek theme that had been left unchanged after the youngster went to college.

"I wish I had updated the room," Eleanor Dvorchak, said. "But he was so congenial, anything would have been fine."[183] Years later, Eleanor recalled that the Chinese leader was calm and intensely focused on learning as much as possible during his brief trip. He kept busy until late each day, so all he needed when he returned in the evening was peace and quiet, she said.

The language barrier made conversation difficult, but she said Xi was interested in touring the home and seemed impressed with the two-car garage and large concrete driveway that had a basketball hoop.

After his return to China, Xi Jinping continued to rise in the political ranks. He served as the governor of Fujian between 1999 and 2002, and then as governor and party secretary of the neighboring province,

Zhejiang, between 2002 and 2007. A pension fund scheme scandal in 2007 led to the dismissal of upper leadership in Shanghai, and Xi was appointed as Shanghai's party secretary. He only held the post for a short period before he was again promoted as one of the nine members of the standing committee of the Chinese Communist Party Political Bureau (Politburo), the highest ruling body in the party. When he was elected vice president of China in March 2008, Xi was assured of being the successor to Hu Jintao, the general secretary of China.

As the heir apparent in the key role of general secretary, Xi was welcomed on trips around the world. During a trade mission to China in September 2011, Governor Branstad met with Vice President Xi in the Great Hall of the People, just off Tiananmen Square, and discussed at length the 1985 Chinese delegation. The vice president informed the governor that he was impressed with the hospitality and friendliness of Iowans and could recall the names of Iowans he had met decades earlier. As a follow-up to their conversation, Governor Branstad sent a letter to Xi, inviting him to visit Iowa again for a reunion of "old friends" from 1985.

On January 23, 2012, the White House announced that Vice President Xi Jinping would visit the United States and make stops in Washington, DC, Iowa, and California. President Obama welcomed Xi to the White House to discuss economic and military relationships, the State Department hosted an elaborate reception, full military honors were given at the Pentagon, and a gathering was held with chief business executives. After his trip on the East Coast concluded, Xi and his delegation continued west for a US–China Agricultural Symposium and to visit his past associates Iowa.

Xi and his entourage first went to Muscatine. Seventeen people he had met on his first trip were invited for tea at the home of the coordinator of the 1985 delegation, Sarah Lande. Also included were Governor Branstad, Muscatine Mayor DeWayne Hopkins, a Chinese delegation of approximately thirty people, and more than a dozen members of the media from both countries. The street in front of the Lande home was blocked, and many townsfolk and curious outsiders gathered to get a glimpse of the vice president.

"I'm flabbergasted that he would take time out of his busy

schedule and come back to Muscatine," said Eleanor Dvorchak. She and her husband had since moved to Florida but made the trip back to Iowa to attend the reunion.[184]

"Coming here is really like coming back home," said Xi. "You can't even imagine what a deep impression I had from my visit 27 years ago to Muscatine, because you were the first group of Americans that I came into contact with. My impression of the country came from you. For me, you are America."[185]

After an hour-long chat, Xi had a photo op with the guests and returned to his motorcade to proceed to Des Moines. There, he was welcomed by Governor Branstad and Lt. Governor Reynolds at an official dinner at the statehouse.

As part of his toast, Governor Branstad said: "We are proud of our mutually beneficial trading partnerships with China, and Iowa farmers are proud to harvest safe and reliable agricultural products for use by the people of China. We hope to build upon these partnerships in related areas where Iowa leads the world, such as biotechnology, advanced manufacturing, food processing, and financial services. We hope this dinner tonight, and your entire visit to Iowa, will foster an even deeper friendship between Iowa and China, one that will continue to grow and benefit both of our peoples.

"In 1985, when you visited me here at the Governor's Office, I was in my late thirties and serving my first term as governor. At that time, you were in your early thirties and a local party leader in Shijiazhuang. I am honored to once again be serving as Iowa's governor and to have this historic opportunity to welcome you back to our state. And so many Iowans are pleased that a man we befriended those many years ago has risen to such a position of prominence and respect in the great nation of China."[186]

The two-day US–China Agricultural Symposium was held at the World Prize Hall of Laureates, beginning on February 16, 2012. The symposium itinerary focused on bilateral cooperation on food safety, food security, and sustainable agriculture, as well as enhanced business relationships between the two countries.

The event included Governor Branstad and former Iowa governor and current US Secretary of Agriculture Tom Vilsack, as well as

Chinese Minister of Agriculture Han Changfu. Xi opened the symposium and stressed the importance China places on supporting farmers and rural development, as well as on food security.

At the conclusion of the symposium an agreement was signed between the US soybean industry and Chinese buyers, who agreed to purchase more than 8.6 million metric tons (317 million bushels) of US soybeans in 2013, totaling approximately $4.3 billion. Governor Branstad compared the significance of Xi's 2012 visit to the 1979 Iowa visit of Pope John Paul II and the 1959 farm stop by Soviet Premier Nikita Khrushchev.

On May 18, 2012, Governor Branstad accepted an invitation from Vice President Xi Jinping to be part of a trade mission to China in 2013 and to celebrate the thirtieth anniversary of the Iowa Sister-State Friendship Committee and the Chinese People's Association for Friendship with Foreign Countries.

On March 14, 2013, Xi Jinping ascended from vice president to the position of general secretary of the Communist Party in China, the president of the People's Republic of China, and chairman of the Central Military Commission. In effect, the move made him one of the most powerful men in the world.

The group of Iowans referred to as "old friends" joined the delegation from Iowa. Aside from the goodwill reunion, Governor Branstad joined Iowa Economic Development Authority Director Debi Durham in meetings to promote Iowa's global partnership and pursue further economic opportunities in Iowa. Other notable members of the delegation included two other governors—Scott Walker of Wisconsin and Bob McDonnell of Virginia, as well as business leaders from John Deere and DuPont Pioneer.

The four-day trip included stops in Beijing, Baoding, and Shijiazhuang in Hebei Province, as well as in Tianjin. The trip also included a celebration of the thirtieth anniversary of the Iowa–Hebei sister-state relationship and a US–China governors forum in Tianjin. A highlight of the trip to China was a "warm and cordial" forty-five-minute conversation with Governor Branstad and President Xi that garnered considerable coverage in the Chinese daily newspapers.

"I greeted him as an old friend, and that's what he calls us. I just felt really good about it," Governor Branstad said. "He specifically talked about the benefit of these sub-national meetings between the provinces and the governors."[187]

During the visit, Governor Branstad wrote an editorial published April 15 in China's official English newspaper, the *China Daily*. "The state of Iowa shares a long economic relationship with the people of China, one that we value and one we want to continue to foster. Our state's safe and reliable agriculture products are an important food source for the Chinese people. In fact, Iowa farmers export more soybeans to China than they do to the rest of the world. It is commonly known in our state that one in every four rows of soybeans eventually makes its way to China.

"On behalf of the farmers of Iowa, we appreciate the chance to be partners with China in our respective countries' economic advancement and ensuring our food security. Our corn and soybeans are vital inputs into China's livestock industries, keeping input prices low, and our pork helps supply Chinese consumers. I can't think of a better example of a win-win partnership."[188]

Nick Compton is an Iowan who at the time was studying at the Global Journalism Institute at a Beijing university, and wrote an opinion piece about the governor's trip that was published in the *Des Moines Register* Voices & Commentary section. The headline declared "Branstad received like a rock star on trip to China" and was accompanied by a photo of Branstad and Xi reaching out to shake hands in the Great Hall of the People in Beijing. It is a remarkable tribute to how far the young boy from Leland had come during his career.

Branstad was standing next to Xi when photographs were taken, and Compton pointed out it was not by accident. "There are 18 officials in the photo but Branstad was assigned to a spot immediately to Xi's right, his Iowa lapel pin nearly rubbing Xi's shoulder. That Branstad is positioned next to Xi, as his right-hand man, is not coincidence. Chinese photo arrangement in group shots is a fine science of status . . . with Xi's loyal endorsement, Branstad and Iowa as a whole, it seems have earned a spot in Beijing's center stage."

Later on, Compton reported the governor was nearly mobbed by enthusiastic Chinese, and one businessman said, "If we have money, we will definitely invest in Iowa."[189]

China was Iowa's second-largest export market in 2013, according to the US-China Business Council, wrote George C. Ford of *The Gazette* in Cedar Rapids. "While $2.3 billion of the $2.9 billion total was from farm commodities, other industries such as aerospace, processed foods and machinery have developed a significant market presence in the world's most prosperous nation.

"'Success in China doesn't happen overnight,' said Colin Mahoney, senior vice president, International and Service Solutions for Rockwell Collins, which has been active in China for more than 30 years. 'You can't parachute in a team to win a particular piece of business and hope that you're going to be better placed than companies that strategically invest in the country. We have tenure and that has given us competitive differentiation.'"[190]

Branstad understands that basic principle of trade and is one of the leaders among the nation's governors who realize the importance of establishing international relationships independent of the federal government. In his six terms to date, he has made an estimated thirty trips out of the country, traveling throughout Europe and Asia in an effort to open markets for Iowa products. He has worked indefatigably to enhance the export ratio heavily in the state's favor.

A headline in the August 11, 2013, issue of the *Des Moines Register's* Opinion section called Branstad "Salesman in chief," even while questioning if such overseas efforts should be the job of any state official. Yet it's a role that the governor relishes and believes it creates goodwill and is vitally important to the state's economic well-being.

CHAPTER ELEVEN

Life in the Bubble

Being the spouse or child of someone who is constantly in the public eye, such as a movie star, premiere athlete, or high-level politician, usually takes a toll on every member of the family in one way or another and to varying degrees. The trials and tribulations of the Kennedys and the Fords are prime examples on the political side, and even Ronald Reagan's family was not immune from scrutiny and some painful episodes.

That was also true of the Branstads after he became governor.

Chris, just thirty years old when they moved into Terrace Hill, was the mother of two young children that she was determined to shield from the public eye. She struggled with the loss of privacy and was forced to stand her ground on a variety of issues, one even involving her mother-in-law. When Rita Branstad came to the mansion and tried to smoke, Chris stopped her, saying it was not allowed. Rita, a heavy smoker, went outside.

One of the most publicized flaps came in 1983 and revolved around the question of how accessible Terrace Hill should be to the public for tours. At one time, Terry Branstad wanted to have the mansion open on Saturdays in addition to the Sunday through Thursday schedule, leaving just Fridays closed to the public. He also wanted the second floor open to the public, instead of just the first floor and the carriage house.

But his plan met stern resistance on the home front. The discussion was taken up by the Terrace Hill Authority, which runs the mansion.

"I don't like giving up my second floor and my weekend," Chris told the group. "I can't give up both days of a weekend and have people milling about." Chris even said she would consider moving to an apartment if the proposals were adopted.[191] A compromise was reached—Terrace Hill remained closed on Saturdays, but the second floor, where the offices of the governor and first lady and guest rooms are located, were opened.

A near-crisis developed in early 1995 when the condition of the mansion reached the point where immediate work was required. It was reported that the Branstads often had to take cold showers because the water pump wasn't working properly, that the electrical wiring needed updating, that the refrigerator was broken, and the elevator needed repairs. To top it all off, a new fire alarm system, valued at near $30,000, was desperately needed.

"If there was fire, we'd all burn up," Chris said.[192]

It was estimated that nearly $400,000 was needed to update the mansion and get everything back in working condition. However, the commission in charge of the mansion had an annual budget of just $175,000. Chris went to the state legislature to request money for fixing up the mansion, and it was awarded.

Still, the most serious problem didn't surface until 2012, and it was truly a "sickening" situation. Chris began feeling uncomfortable in July, and her health got worse. "I got really sick, the sickest I have ever been in my life," she said two years later. "I even lost my sense of taste and smell.

"We were going to South America on a trade mission. While we were gone, I asked that an air quality study be done on Terrace Hill." The study showed that there was a very serious black mold problem on the third floor, where the living quarters are. The walls had to be taken down to the studs, and the entire third floor was rebuilt. A capital campaign, state maintenance funds, and additional state appropriations were all used in the renovation. The work began in September, and Chris was anxious to have it completed by Thanksgiving.

"There were about twenty-five people in here working," she said. "They were the nicest people and did such a great job. They wanted the remodel to be a surprise for us. When we came in and saw what they had done, I just started bawling. And I haven't been sick since."[193]

Renovations included lighting on the grounds, steps at the south entry, HVAC/geothermal upgrades, a kitchen upgrade, mold remediation, and window replacement; oriental rug repair and restoration; repairs to the main portico; east porch repairs and a security gate arm replacement. In total, $4.2 million was spent on the renovations.

During Branstad's third term as governor, his wife, at age thirty-nine, made a monumental decision about her own life when she enrolled at DMAAC. After finding out that some of her hours from the University of Iowa years transferred, she set out to get her associate degree in the medical assistant program.

"It just clicked—something in my brain said I was going to do it. I hadn't had a paid job in seventeen years, and that was my choice," she said. "But I decided I had to do this now or never. I drove to Ankeny for classes; it took me over a year. I celebrated my fortieth birthday at DMACC and was hired that September."[194]

She worked full time at a family medical practice for two years, then at a plastic surgery office for three years, followed by a short stint in a family practice office in Polk City.

"I had to work," she said with a shrug. "We had two kids in college and one in Catholic school. But I was happy. I really, really loved working." She said she developed her affection for the medical profession back on the Winnebago County farm when they were first married, and she was giving shots to baby pigs. "I love giving shots," she said in an AP interview. "The ultimate compliment is when a patient tells me that it didn't hurt."[195]

On February 20, 1994, the Lifestyle section of the *Des Moines Register* had featured a lengthy article called "Running Mates," focusing on the spouses of the three major candidates for governor. Catherine Mann, the wife of Grandy, had a long, extensive career in the public eye as a television talk show host and novelist. Ed Campbell was profiled as a tough, no-nonsense type of guy who had survived both cancer and alcoholism and had earned a reputation as a top Democratic consultant on a national level.

Chris was portrayed as a devoted mother and wife who had struggled to come to terms with being in the public eye, and had been successful in that endeavor.

"She is not the same Chris Branstad who moved into the governor's mansion eleven years ago," wrote Phoebe Wall Howard. "Branstad accepts life in the fishbowl. Her perspective on life seems to have changed. She cares less about what the public thinks of her. 'Maybe it's age,' she said, laughing."[196]

The biggest changes came with the demands of raising a family and also building a career of her own. Mornings were filled with the routine of getting the children off to school and then going to work herself. Though she had a driver at her beck and call, she always drove the kids to school, preferring to keep the common touch in their lives. She told Howard that she would not allow her husband's passion and profession to dominate her role.

"I'm interested in politics, but it's not my life. My life has changed in the past two and half years . . . Now my life is my job, my kids and my husband. That's it."[197]

In 1999, Allison Branstad, then age twenty-one and a college senior, confided to columnist Rob Borsellino that life in Terrace Hill had its tough moments—such as when lying in the sun in a swimming suit at a young age and a tour group came through, staring at her; or when boys wanted to come calling but were intimidated by all the security around the mansion. She admitted the mansion is so big that she got lost a few times early on (she was five when they moved in), and even got her arm caught in the door of the elevator, which doesn't happen in too many homes.

And then there was the constant media glare. "You've got to watch your back," Allison said. "My brother's a good example of that. I wasn't a party animal, but I'm not an angel. I did the normal things and I was lucky I never got caught."[198]

In an interview in 1996, Terry Branstad took a good, hard look at his successes and failures as governor. He also spoke briefly about the demands of the job and how it could have impacted his family time.

"Branstad acknowledges the demands of the job have forced him to give up much of his private life," wrote Thomas A. Fogarty for the *Des Moines Register*. "'It does take away from your family. There's no question about that,' said Branstad, the father of three. 'I've always tried to tell my kids you've got to accept the bad with the good. You give up privacy. You're very much a public person. And yet (the children) get the chance to meet presidents and other governors, and go to conferences and things like that.'"[199]

The governor has endured his share of frightening moments over the years. There were the three plane flights that could have wound up in tragedy, including the one on October 30, 1978, in Sioux City when the landing gear froze and the plane was forced to make a belly landing, skidding to a halt on the runaway.

Exactly one year later, on the morning of October 30, while returning from a speech in Mason City, he was involved in an accident on his way back to Lake Mills. A truck driven by a local resident pulled in front of his car; Branstad applied the brakes, but his car went under the side of the truck and was totaled. He sustained rib injuries and struck his head on the windshield and was taken to Mercy hospital to have a piece of glass removed from his skull. The other driver was charged with failing to yield the right of way at a stop sign.

In May 1988, the governor was questioned about his belief in astrology after it was reported in the media that Nancy Reagan had consulted astrologers while in the White House to see if the stars were aligned favorably. "Even on the 30th of October, a day in which I have had two accidents, I still work," he said. When asked what sign he was, Branstad confessed he had no idea and didn't care.

"That's news to me," he said when told he was a Scorpio. "I don't know what I am. I'm a Republican, I'm the governor of Iowa, my mother gave me the name of Terry. That's about all I know. I can answer tough questions, but I don't know anything about astrology. I'm sorry."[200]

Yet another time, he and Doug Gross were flying to a destination when heavy fog set it. The pilot seemed a bit flummoxed, said Gross, and "pulled out a flight manual, turning to the page that explained how to fly in fog. That was a bit unsettling."[201]

Contrary to what many people may think, the governor does not have his own plane or charter service. Whenever he wants to fly somewhere, a staff member has to try and find someone who will donate the time and finances (and plane) to take him.

However, the most unusual accident occurred on January 17, 1993, when he and his eight-year-old son Marcus went sledding on a hill at Waveland Golf Course. On one run, he was hit by a sled and broke bones in his face. He was taken to a hospital for treatment, his face swollen and bruised. His jaw was broken and, after surgery, was wired shut for a month. "I guess maybe I'm too old to go sledding," he said.

He had been scheduled to leave the next day for the inauguration of the new president-elect, Bill Clinton, in Washington, DC, but cancelled the trip. Though he was slowed down considerably by the injury, he showed his innate toughness once again by his rapid recovery.

"Terry Branstad's shattered jaw has been freed, and he's hit the road with a vengeance," reported the AP on February 19, 1993. "Branstad immediately left on a barnstorming tour that had been stalled by broken bones the governor suffered in a sledding accident. The wires were cut four weeks after surgeons repaired six broken bones in Branstad's face, a relatively brief recovery. Doctors had estimated his jaw could be wired shut for as long as six weeks.

"Some metal does remain in Branstad's face, helping to hold things in line, but the governor now can speak normally," said his spokesman Richard Vohs.[202]

Branstad may have been the youngest man ever elected governor in Iowa, but his son Marcus made his mark too. When he arrived on January 22, 1984, he became the first baby born to an Iowa governor since Ansel Briggs and his wife had a daughter in 1847. The Branstad family resided on the third floor, and because there was no nursery in the living quarters, a sitting room off the master bedroom was converted to serve as one.

In 1996, Marcus decided he would like to live on the Branstad family farm near Leland for a year, and his parents allowed him to do so. He had attended a Catholic school in Des Moines through the first six grades, but in 1996–97 he was in the same school district in Forest City that his father had graduated from.

"He's having a good time," the governor said. "He's learned to drive all the tractors. And they've got a lot of cattle to take care of up there." Eric Woolson, Branstad's press secretary, added that it was an opportunity for Marcus to be in an environment with less attention on his father's job and just be a kid. Eric and Alison were already away from home in college, so Chris and Terry Branstad became "empty nesters" at the time.

"Ask Chris Branstad how she describes herself and one word keeps popping up: normal. And back in 1999, after the Branstads moved out of Terrace Hill, Chris Branstad couldn't wait to take her husband back and be normal again," wrote Reid Forgrave in 2010. "She soon learned you can take the man out of politics but you can't take the politics out of the man."[203]

In 2012, they bought a home on Lake Panorama, a private area located west of Des Moines. It was developed after the Middle Raccoon River was dammed up in 1970, and today includes a 1,400-acre lake for boating and offers private beaches, a fitness center, two golf courses, tennis courts, and more. With 1,750 property owners, it is the largest private lake in the state. "We go out there a lot and really enjoy it," said Chris Branstad. "As far as what Terry does in his leisure time, history and sports are Terry's two loves; he doesn't really have any hobbies."[204]

They both are concerned about staying active, especially after Terry Branstad suffered a minor heart attack in 2000. He and his wife had worked out at the YMCA in the morning, and when they came out of the building, he got sick. He was in the hospital for several days and had a stent put in to help the blood flow. He was back at work in less than a week, and in 2010 another stent was added.

Just two years later, he was saddened by the loss of longtime friend and running partner Mel Straub, who died of cancer in February 2002. Straub founded a highly successful printing company in 1971 that bears his name, and he and his wife, Jan, were strong supporters of the governor as well as close friends. Mel Straub had worked closely with John Ruan in establishing the John Ruan Multiple Sclerosis Golf Classic. Today, Jan Straub is president and CEO of Straub Corporation in Des Moines.

Terry and Chris can often be seen at Gray's Lake, walking briskly in the early morning several times a week. They also spend time at the wellness center at Des Moines University in the winter and when the weather is bad. But still, he reserves most of his energy for the job that he loves. And he has an amazing amount of energy to give to the position, according to those who have worked for him through the years.

Matt Hinch, a graduate of Des Moines Dowling Catholic High School and University of Iowa, served as chief of staff during the 2014 election period and brought a wide range of experience to the job. He had previously worked on Capitol Hill in Washington, DC, from 2003 to 2009, and then took a positon in the Iowa House Republican Caucus and the Des Moines Partnership. He has the highest regard for the commitment to service of almost all politicians, and Branstad in particular.

"His work ethic is remarkable," said Hinch after the election. "Just last week he was telling me about locking himself in the law library at night when he was serving in the legislature so he could study. Even now his public schedule is unbelievable. He is always wanting us to add things to it.

"He is truly a selfless public official. . . . It is never about him, it's always about what is best for the state of Iowa. He is probably the most accessible elected official I have ever come across, and I've known quite a few good ones."[205]

Hinch also admires Branstad's determination to be fully prepared. He recalled an important event in Washington, DC, when Branstad was cochairman of a subcommittee that was meeting at the Pentagon to discuss additional funding for state National Guard units. Branstad was sitting across from Secretary of Defense Chuck Hagel and in the company of the head of Homeland Security, the Joint Chiefs of Staff, and six other governors. The meeting had its tense moments.

"Governor Branstad went toe-to-toe with Hagel and did a phenomenal job of fighting for funding," said Hinch. "You could tell the other governors really appreciated what he was doing and respected him.

"It all goes back to preparation. He works very hard to be prepared for these kinds of meetings and for everything he does."[206]

A characteristic that Hinch feels has served Branstad well is his calm under pressure. "You don't get as far as he has without being able to take all the criticism with a grain of salt. He is really unflappable." That can apply to attacks in the media or to overly excited citizens in public.

Once when attending an Iowa football game in 2013, Branstad and his small group were standing at the elevator door on the top floor inside the press box, waiting to leave as the game was winding down. Another dozen or so spectators were also waiting for the elevator, and one of the men, probably in his thirties, spotted the governor. It was obvious the fellow had been drinking, and he began talking loudly about the governor in an obnoxious manner and tone.

It took so long for the elevator to arrive that the governor and his group started down the stairway, and the others all followed, including the boisterous fan. He kept shouting, "Hey, Jerry Branstad, or whatever your name is, I want to talk to ya" all the way down. Once outside, the governor kept moving toward his SUV, stopping to chat briefly with fans who spotted him and wanted to shake his hand. The boisterous fan soon was lost in the huge crowd.

Finally settled in the backseat of the vehicle, one of the other men in the small group turned to the governor. "Did you hear that loudmouth?" he asked. "He was really out of line the way he kept shouting your name."

The governor shrugged and smiled. "You get used to that sort of thing," he said. "You just pretend like you don't hear and keep moving. It doesn't happen very often, and when it does, it doesn't bother me at all."[207]

Branstad seeks out and respects candid feedback from his staff members, said Hinch. "I've had very frank conversations with him and tell him the unvarnished truth. He takes it all in, very calmly, very thoughtfully, then makes his decision and moves on."[208]

The ability to keep moving forward despite any setbacks, big or small, has been a characteristic that has served Branstad well for decades.

CHAPTER TWELVE

THE LEGACY

Perhaps longevity is Terry Branstad's greatest legacy, as it is what people will remember first and talk about the most. After all, we are a nation that loves to rank our heroes, and the Leland native stands tall on the list of the longest serving governors in both Iowa history and American history. In that regard, he is the Babe Ruth of Iowa politics, the man who those yet to come will be measured against.

But there is a lot more, of course, depending on who is talking.

"I spent thirty years trying to beat him, and now I'm supporting him," said Des Moines real estate legend Bill Knapp, in 2013. Knapp has been a major player on the Democratic side of Iowa politics for decades but backed Branstad in the 2014 election. "Maybe I don't agree with everything Terry does, but I sure admire his love of the state and his devotion to it. I've become a fan."[209]

Henry Tippie is a native of Belle Plaine who served in World War II in the South Pacific and graduated from the University of Iowa in 1949 with a degree in accounting. He has been tremendously successful in the business world and has been a huge supporter of the University of Iowa. Today, students can attend the Henry B. Tippie College of Business and School of Management. He owns a 33,000-acre ranch in Limestone, Texas, and an entire wing of the Belle Plaine Museum is named in his honor. Tippie met Branstad twenty-five years ago while working on a project with Lee Lieu, who at the time was CEO and president of Iowa Electric Light and Power, headquartered in Cedar Rapids.

"I believe Iowa has been very fortunate to have Terry Branstad as governor," said Tippie in 2015. "The thing that impresses me so much is that he works hard at being governor—he isn't using the position as a stage for some higher office. And I think the people of Iowa get that.

"It's also very impressive that he tries to visit all ninety-nine counties every year. Who else would do something like that? He's been extremely important to Iowa. He's worked very hard at being governor. When you're in politics you can't expect everyone to agree with all that you do, but I believe the people of Iowa respect him and what he's done."[210]

It's an opinion shared by nearly all who have worked closely with the governor, including Jeff Boeyink. "This governor doesn't have any personal agenda—except for the state of Iowa to do well. None of it is a facade; people may not always agree with him, but they know he's sincere."[211]

Mike Glover of the Associated Press wrote about the Branstad legacy back in 1998, and framed it thus: "The first and most obvious conclusion that can be drawn is that the primary legacy of Branstad's tenure in office is political in nature. Branstad has proven to be a far tougher—and smarter—politician than his critics believe."[212]

"Is he the best politician in state history?" asked Doug Gross rhetorically. "Absolutely, not even close. In every respect he embodies Iowa. One of the amazing things is that he has never acted haughty or egotistical in any way whatsoever. He doesn't need to be the smartest guy in the room—he just wants to have the smartest guys in the room so he can get their advice and learn from them. And he is a great salesman; Terry Branstad can sell anything, and what he loves to sell the most is Iowa."[213]

Susan Neely supports that analysis: "Terry has always been a very self-confident man. One of the ways this confidence manifests itself is in his willingness to enlist smart people with diverse points of view and skills. From his first run for state office as lieutenant governor, to 1982, 1986, and beyond, I can reel off names of special people who worked on his campaign staff or in volunteer leadership who were extraordinary individuals in their own right.

"There are dozens of former staff who went on to very successful careers. From my own standpoint, I don't hesitate to credit my service to the governor as foundational to other professional successes. When I worked for him, he was in his midthirties and I in my midtwenties. As I watched his sharp campaign staff on election night in 2014, I was impressed that even though he is in his midsixties now, he is still smart enough to surround himself with the best and brightest in their twenties or thirties.

"On the surface, Terry may seem like an unlikely person to have run for political office. He's not the stereotypical, slick, telegenic candidate out of Hollywood central casting. In fact, he is the opposite of 'slick' in all the good ways. First and foremost, he has a deep respect for the people he serves. He doesn't have to speak first or suck all the oxygen out of the room, filling it with his own point of view as a way to appear important.

"He is humble by nature and is sometimes understated in injecting his opinion into a group discussion. In part, this is because he is listening to and actively considering or learning from other points of view . . . again an atypical attribute for those who enter political life. Of course, being understated can sometimes yield a competitive advantage in politics. A friend of mine in Washington who is a national operative for Democratic candidates has said that the state of Iowa is littered with people who have underestimated Terry Branstad in past elections.

"Until they know Terry, people don't always realize that he is a serious policy wonk. He has close to a photographic memory and can recall facts, figures, names, places, and dates with ease. This is a very useful skill in politics and can even create a 'wow' factor when he'll remind someone of the place and time when he met them, and then follow up with a question about their family, business, or community."[214]

"If he has an Achilles' heel, it is how trusting he can sometimes be," said Lyle Simpson, an adviser who has been with him for nearly four decades. "He generally believes in people. He's very smart and a quick study, but he can also be a bit malleable at times."[215]

But his many strengths overshadow any weaknesses, in the opinion of most Iowans. They proved it at the polls numerous times over several decades, and many media experts seem in agreement.

"Branstad's legacy is just fine even with a package that falls short of his vision; he came in with the beginnings of a farm crisis that rocked the state, and he will leave it with historic cash balances and tax trimming," declared the *Storm Lake Pilot Tribune* in 1998 after the end of Branstad's sixteen-year run.

"If he will be remembered as the governor for Iowa's disgraceful era of pandering to gambling, he will also be remembered for Iowa's era of economic development.

"If he will be remembered for Iowa's controversial response to huge hog lots, he will also be remembered for a laudable commitment to Iowa's schools."[216]

And of course, there was the work ethic that he brought to Des Moines from his father's farm back in his Leland days. During his last year in his first run as governor, in 1997, David Yepsen captured that spirit when he wrote an article for the *Des Moines Register*: "Terry Branstad didn't get to be Iowa's longest serving governor by missing political opportunities. Nor did he get there by taking it easy. He doesn't plan to let up in his last year in office.

"'I'm a workhorse. That's the way I grew up. So I intend to work hard every day until I leave this office. I want to accomplish as much as I can as governor.'"[217]

"He's taken the state from chaos to solvency twice," said Doug Gross. "That's quite a legacy right there."[218]

Even some Democrats have to admit that during the time Branstad has been governor again, from 2010 to 2014, the state's financial well-being has improved dramatically.

"A perfect credit rating and strong budget make Iowa one of the best run states in the country," said Iowa State Senator Jeff Danielson in an e-mail sent to his constituents on September 18, 2014. "I am proud of the bipartisan efforts of the Legislature to balance the state budget without raising taxes and set aside money for a rainy day. We use caution when determining how much to spend by looking at recent revenue estimates from a nonpartisan panel of experts and budgeting in a conservative manner.

"With this approach, Iowa is expected to have a budget surplus of about $735 million when this fiscal year ends on June 30, 2015. We also have $696 million in our Cash Reserves and Economic Emergency funds, the largest amount in state history. These rainy day funds—equal to about 10 percent of our state budget—are among the strongest in the country, according to the Tax Foundation."

He added that Mary Mosiman, the state auditor, "noted Iowa's strong fiscal condition in her review this summer of state finances. 'Not only has the spending gap been reduced to $171 million,' she said, 'but we now have a surplus of almost $750 million, in addition to our reserve funds, which are full. The fiscal discipline of the last few years is paying off, and we need to ensure it continues."

Danielson said that "Iowa consistently earns the best possible rating from Standard and Poor's, which means the state has an extremely strong capacity to meet financial commitments in full and on time. This strong credit rating, in addition to our well-managed budget and low debt, put Iowa among the top three best-run states in the nation, according to 24/7 Wall Street."[219]

It was an unintentional testimonial to the strong and dedicated work of a Republican governor who has spent his entire political career preaching about fiscal responsibility and working with the other side of the aisle to take strong and decisive action to support his beliefs. Largely because of the leadership of Terry Branstad, Iowa has moved to the front of the line when it comes to financial security.

"His persistence, work habits, and his love for the state of Iowa are his legacy," said David Fisher. "And that radiates to the citizens of Iowa. He can go into a community and talk about their new fire station—and they love that. They know that he really cares.

"Every spring I put on an event here at the Des Moines Club, and we invite all the graduating senior athletes from the University of Iowa and the various coaches," said Fisher. "It's an excellent opportunity for them to meet business leaders. The governor comes every year and does an outstanding job of telling these outstanding young people to stay in Iowa. The years he was governor he came every time . . . and when he was out of office we could not get the other governors to come one time."[220]

Neely also pointed out that her former boss has a strong record of supporting women through the appointment and electoral process. "It would be interesting to run the numbers, but I suspect he may have had more women in his administrations than any other governor," she said in 2015. "He appointed the first woman to the Iowa Supreme Court. He has had female running mates on multiple occasions. Through his female general counsel in the first term, he triggered a review of the state code to eliminate sexist references. He also supported a commission on comparable worth to review pay equity."[221]

Joy Corning is one of many who have benefitted from Branstad's commitment to an inclusive administration and is deeply appreciative of the opportunity that Branstad offered to her back in 1990. More than two decades later, she spoke with unabashed admiration for her former boss.

"Governor Branstad loves politics and loves the state of Iowa," she said quietly in 2014. "He loves being governor, and so I wasn't totally shocked when he decided to come back." She paused. "I feel absolutely so privileged to have been chosen to be his lieutenant governor. It was a marvelous experience."[222]

In 2010, Kim Reynolds found herself in the same position as Joy Corning. What has impressed her besides the knowledge and expertise that Branstad has gained over the decades in high office is the way both he and Chris Branstad have handled their positions as governor and first lady.

"His love for the state is immeasurable, and he's very fun to work with. We work very hard, but we also have fun. His schedule is incredible, and people love to see him. But he and Chris are so humble, and I think people sense that about them. He is soooo approachable; people are very comfortable coming up to him, young and old, and chatting."[223]

One of many common bonds between the two is their shared commitment to education on all levels. She has been a huge advocate of the STEM (which stresses science, technology, engineering, and math) program for high school students and cochairs the governor's advisory committee on STEM. Each year, she visits all ninety-nine counties in the state, something her boss has done every year since becoming governor.

While assessing Branstad's legacy, it should be noted that following in the footsteps of such a popular governor as Robert Ray was not easy. Ask coaches who followed in the footsteps of Vince Lombardi at Green Bay, John Wooden of UCLA, or Dan Gable at Iowa how easy it was trying to live up to such lofty achievements and expectations.

Ray had, according to one insider, two traits that made him so successful: He was a very intelligent person with great leadership capacity; and he never spoke out on any issues until he knew where the parade was going. While Ray was a directive type of leader, Branstad was more inclined to hire good people and let them go do their thing. He's not a micro manager and is interested in new ideas, according to Tim Albrecht, who served as his communications director from 2009 to 2013.

Even though he was born and raised in Ida Grove, the hometown of Harold Hughes, one of the most respected governors in Iowa history and a staunch Democrat, Albrecht's parents were conservative, laying the foundation for his political philosophy. He was hired in 2009 by Governor Branstad to spearhead the social media program, an area in which the governor admittedly was not well informed.

"He was very impressed that young people were responsive to social media techniques, and he was fascinated by that," said Albrecht in 2014. "He's great to work for because he doesn't micro manage, he just tells you what he'd like to accomplish and then lets you go do it. Terry Branstad is someone who is not afraid to try new things and to put people around him who have new ideas. He doesn't surround himself with 'yes people' because he really wants to find solutions.

"He also inspires loyalty because he's such a good person that you don't want to let him down."[224]

Like nearly everyone else who worked for Branstad, Albrecht was impressed with his sincere affection for the state he was elected to govern.

"I remember once we were at a small town on the Mississippi River, I really can't remember which one because we were all over the state on a campaign trip. We were at a very nice house and walked out onto the back deck; we could see all along the Mississippi River. The governor stood there gazing out over the land for quite some time, then said, 'This is the most beautiful view in the world.' And that's from someone who has traveled all around the world. He genuinely loves this state. And his work ethic is astounding. He never seems to get tired."[225]

Another young man who knows firsthand how hard the governor works is Jimmy Centers, a twenty-eight-year-old who has been his communications director since 2013.

"His energy is amazing," said Centers. "There are some young people like me who travel with him, and we can hardly keep his pace. He's like a machine. When he is campaigning, he will often give five speeches a day. He talks for about twenty minutes then opens it up for questions. He spends time between stops going over the issues in each town and really studies. There is no prescreening of questions; people can ask anything they want, so he really has to be on his toes, and he almost always hits it out of the park.

"One time this year (2014), we were in Waterloo, and we were dog-tired after a long, tough day. The next morning I was still tired and was moving slowly. All of us were. Then I saw the governor . . . he was raring to get going already. It's amazing; he's like the Energizer Bunny. I've never seen him have a down day."

Centers estimated that the governor made nearly 2,500 public event appearances in 2014. "The man just loves Iowa, and he loves meeting people. He never stops learning about the state and things about it. He's an Iowa encyclopedia."[226]

Certainly, his remarkable ability to retain details is a key to his success as a politician who can connect with people, but it can also lead him astray on occasion.

"Sometimes his fascination with and knowledge of policy specifics may cause him to delve into more detail than a lay audience really wants to hear," said Susan Neely in 2014, from her office in Washington, DC. "When I heard him speak on the campaign trail in 2010 after years in private life, there was a subtle moment in the middle of his detailed answer on the state of Iowa's accounting system when he must have realized that he was getting too much into the weeds. He made an almost imperceptible pause before he quickly summarized with his main point.

"The moment was vintage Terry Branstad. And regardless of whether the people in that room needed to know all those details, they could leave reassured that they would have a governor who knew what he was talking about."[227]

Visitors to the Iowa Hall of Pride in Des Moines can hear the governor talking firsthand about his life. In the lavish facility, director Jack Lashier has worked indefatigably to build a lasting tribute to the men and women of all ages and backgrounds who have helped shape the state's history on many levels. In the center of the huge facility is an interactive exhibit called "Iowans," featuring Branstad talking candidly about nineteen different areas of his life, ranging from his days on the farm at Leland to his high school years to his legacy as governor. Just twenty feet away is the gorgeous exhibit dedicated to the career of legendary pianist Roger Williams, and visitors can press a button and listen to his best-selling recordings of "Autumn Leaves," "Somewhere In Time," and "Born Free."

Though now firmly entrenched in the Iowa Hall of Pride and the state's history, Branstad's success wasn't obvious to everyone at the outset of his career. Ken Sullivan served as political editor of *The Gazette* in Cedar Rapids from 1980 through 2001 and has been a keen observer of the Iowa political scene for over three decades.

"Frankly, I'm surprised at his durability and the long-term success," said Sullivan in 2014. "Looking back at the legislators when Terry came in, he wouldn't have been the person I would have thought would wind up setting a record for most years as governor, that's for sure."[228]

Sullivan said he felt Branstad had some drawbacks and wasn't a dynamic speaker but was able to overcome those deficiencies through plain hard work and discipline. "He knew that (speaking in public) was a shortcoming, and he really worked hard at it and improved through the years," said Doug Gross. "I think a lot of Iowans could relate to that and have empathy for him in that respect."[229]

"Both Terry Branstad and Chuck Grassley have really mastered the skill of textbook politics," said Sullivan. "Branstad came into the office at a bad time, with the farm crisis and everything. He was a Herbert Hoover type in that regard. But he's been a good administrator, and as a politician he has a lot more plusses than negatives.

"God bless him . . . and others who go into politics. It's a really tough job, and it's gotten even more so now than it was twenty, thirty years ago. Thank goodness someone is willing to do it."[230]

On January 9, 2014, popular WHO radio talk show host Jan Mickelson made an offhand remark that probably sums up the success of the Leland native as succinctly as possible: "Terry Branstad is probably the best politician in the history of the state," said Michelson. "He reads the public mood better than anyone else ever has."

Indeed, the record seems to bear out that statement.

CHAPTER THIRTEEN

Reflections

One of the truly essential elements to building a successful political career is to bring loyal and hardworking people into the campaign and, ultimately, into the governing process itself. Ever since he first made the decision to enter politics, Terry Branstad has displayed the ability to attract dedicated workers and to keep them involved for long periods of time, either on staff or as supporters when they have moved on to other positions.

And no one fits that role better than Margaret Hough, the woman who has been at his side for two decades. "Margaret—she's a key in all of this," said David Fisher with an admiring shake of the head. "She's been at his side for a long time, through most of his governor years, then at Des Moines University, now back in the governor's office."[231]

"She's the best thing that ever happened to him (at the office)," said Lyle Simpson in a matter-of-fact tone. "It's almost a maternal type of thing."[232]

"Margaret is the governor's keeper," said Tim Albrecht. "She makes sure the train is running on time. She has worked for him long enough that she understands him very well."[233]

Margaret John was born into a family of eleven children in Modale, Iowa, a tiny village about the same size as Leland, located in the far western part of the state in Harrison County. She also knew about hard work from observing her parents; her father ran a small grocery store, and her mother took care of the family brood. After high school, Margaret had a scholarship to attend Dana College in Nebraska, about twenty-five miles northwest of Omaha, but opted instead to work at a bank back home, where she remained for twelve years.

She married Leo Hough, and they moved to Harlan, where they owned a floral shop and Leo found work as the director of the chamber of commerce and economic development. In 1989, Governor Branstad met Leo and offered him a job in his administration as bureau chief. At a birthday party for Branstad, Margaret heard that the governor was looking for a fundraiser for his 1990 campaign. She thought it sounded like an exciting job and expressed an interest, and she was hired too. She performed so well that Branstad brought her into the administration to advise him on appointments of people to boards and commissions. Soon she was handling a variety of tasks and organized the gubernatorial inaugurations. She pulled them off with flair and precision, and always on budget.

"Iowans put on their glad rags and dancing shoes Friday and from morning til midnight celebrated the fourth inauguration of Gov. Terry Branstad," wrote Chuck Offenburger in his column, "Iowa Boy," on January 18, 1995. "About 1,700 attended swearing in ceremonies Friday morning at Veterans Memorial Auditorium, which by nightfall inaugural director Margaret Hough had somehow turned into a huge, elegant ballroom—complete with three huge chandeliers, fresh flowers everywhere, and a fountain 30 feet wide with eight spewing water jets in the middle of the floor. Hough estimated the crowd at the ball at 4,000 or more."[234]

It doesn't take long being around Margaret to understand that she is very good at what she does, whatever it is, and that she keeps things moving smoothly. She said it's because the entire staff is motivated to do the best they can for a boss who works so hard and deserves their respect. She also gives credit to people she worked with in years past.

"Dick Redman was my boss and one of my mentors," she said in 2014, sitting in the governor's office in the Iowa State Capitol. "We had great people running the place. We worked a lot of sixty-hour weeks during campaign time, but no one ever complained because the governor was there working too. We would often be in small planes, eating on the run. Once we flew to a funeral in a Blackhawk helicopter, with open windows. It was hot and noisy."[235]

One of the most memorable trips came in late 1997, when Governor Branstad was in New York City to speak on behalf of Lamar Alexander, who was running for a presidential nomination, and was then supposed to go to Florida to speak at the Republican Governors Convention. But they received word that septuplets had been born to a couple from Carlisle at the Iowa Methodist Medical Center and Blank Memorial Hospital for Children in Des Moines, and the governor felt he needed to be back in Iowa.

The event attracted worldwide attention; President Bill Clinton called from the White House to talk to the stunned couple, Kenny and Bobbi McCaughey. The parents even made the cover of *Time* magazine.

"We flew back from New York, and the governor went out to Methodist Hospital for a press conference," said Margaret Hough. "Those septuplets (four girls and three boys) were very important to the governor. At three a.m. the next morning, we were back in a plane on our way to the Republican Governors Convention in Miami. George W. Bush and Mike Huckabee were speakers there too. When I got back home, someone said to me, 'I'll bet you enjoyed shopping in Miami.' I said, 'Why would you go shopping when you could listen to all these men talk about education and other important issues?'"[236]

There are many other events that she fondly recalls. During the 1990 election, the staff received word that President George H. W. Bush was going to fly in on Air Force One. The ballroom was overbooked, and the Secret Service was upset when they found out that there were frustrated people outside wanting to get in.

"President Bush spoke, and that was quite an experience itself," she said. "When Margaret Thatcher came in 1991, I was in awe of her. Her husband came with her, and Buena Vista College hosted them one night. It was really wonderful.

"Lots of big names were coming in on a regular basis. It was very exciting and interesting."[237]

When Branstad decided not to run again and Tom Vilsack became the new governor in 1999, Leo Hough lost his position and took a job at Drake University as a fundraiser, helping to finance the renovation of Drake Stadium. Margaret Hough went with Branstad to his new job as president of Des Moines University, working in his office there. And when he returned to the governor's office in 2010, the Houghs came back too. Margaret serves as special assistant to the governor while Leo is office manager, coordinating all the incoming phone calls and, as he says with a smile, "finding out who's mad about what."[238]

The office of a governor is a beehive of activity with a wide spectrum of people wanting a few minutes of the governor's time, to talk about whatever issue is most important to them. Maintaining a tight schedule is imperative for everyone concerned, and it's not always easy to keep the governor on track if he is enjoying a conversation with someone and others are lined up at the door waiting to get in, but Margaret Hough seems adept at handling it all with aplomb. It's a skill that no doubt has been cultivated through years of experience.

But even she can get a bit frazzled during the final days of a bruising campaign. Each of the administration staff is assigned a city to travel to for the final two days to work the phones and get voters out of their homes and to the polls. She particularly recalls the tension in the 1994 primary with Fred Grandy.

"I was in Council Bluffs for the final two days working on absentee ballots, rushed back to Des Moines on Election Day, changed clothes, then hurried to the Marriott to wait for the results," she said. "I was a little nervous, actually. We didn't know we had won until later in the evening."[239]

Even a governor with an undefeated track record can get uptight on Election Day, say those closest to him. According to Branstad's friends, as the day wears on he tries to stay close to his wife, as she has the ability to keep him grounded. When the election is finally over, he likes to take a vacation to unwind and recharge his battery, usually with a couple with whom they are close friends.

After his first election for governor they went to San Francisco. Following the second election, it was off to Hawaii, and following the third election, they went to Paris for ten days and also visited the beaches at Normandy, where the Allied troops came ashore on

D-Day, June 6, 1944, to begin the liberation of Europe from Nazi Germany. In 1997, they went to Alaska on their twenty-fifth wedding anniversary.

"In Paris, we were at the Louvre when a young woman spotted him and came running over, all excited," said Lyle Simpson. "She was from Iowa and said she just had to have her picture taken with him. Then, on the same trip at dinner, a woman kept looking at him and finally came over, saying, 'Oh my gosh, it's Governor Branstad.' He is really good with people at times like that and will talk with them for a long time."[240]

When the Branstads and the Simpsons were touring Egypt, two women from Iowa spotted him when they were in front of the great Sphinx and came right over to greet him. "He stood there talking with them for the longest time, with his back to the Sphinx," laughed Simpson. "But that's Terry—he just loves people and he loves talking about Iowa, anywhere in the world."[241]

His style was noticed and appreciated by Henry B. Tippie, the Belle Plaine native who became very successful in the business world and has lived most of his adult life in Texas. "Every time I've been with him, I always felt very comfortable, and I think that's because he's so comfortable in his own clothes. He knows who he is and what he's trying to do. He's middle America and doesn't try to be something other than what he is."[242]

While walking, reading, and watching sports are the main forms of relaxation for Branstad, he remembers that Robert Ray had one particular, rather unique, way of relaxing.

"Bob had a table tennis set up in the office space and would often take on staff members in highly competitive table tennis games," said Terry with a smile, relishing the image of the state's governmental leader banging away with a ping-pong racket in his hand. "He was very good. That's not a technique I picked up from him, though.

"What I learned from Robert Ray was the technique of running the office and how he treated people," said Branstad. "He made you like him and want to set a good example when working for him. Bob would sometimes come in early in the morning, work past lunch then take the afternoon off. He would come back later and work into the evening. He'd make a lot of calls at night. Maybe he would get some letters criticizing him for a certain decision, and he would pick up the phone and call them and say, 'Hi, this is Governor Ray, and I got your letter . . .' And they would have a good discussion. He won a lot of people over by doing that, and I was always intrigued by that.

"I do it sometimes, but not as much as Bob did."[243]

Still, according to those who know him best, Branstad is a master at building relationships that will come back to serve him. "He believes in building bridges," said Matt Hinch, his chief of staff in 2014–15. "The more bridges you build and the friendships you create, the better you are. It's a philosophy that has served him well."[244]

Nowhere was that style more evident than in 2012 when Branstad reached out to Bill Knapp, perhaps the single biggest donor to Democratic politics in Iowa history. Branstad invited Knapp and his top partners, Bill Knapp II and Gerry Neugent, to the governor's office to discuss various ways of working together.

"There was some tension between the two old adversaries as the meeting started, and Bill addressed it directly, telling Branstad, 'I was impressed getting a call from you because you know how much I've personally spent to keep you out of office.' Branstad acknowledged the statement and said he knew they could not agree on social issues but hoped to find common ground."[245]

What resulted was the Skilled Iowa Initiative program, which was largely funded by generous donations from Knapp and others he brought into the fold. The fact that the two powerful men, one from the political world and the other from the private sector, could put aside their differences and develop a strong program that would help create jobs was a resounding success and helped cement their personal relationship as well.

"It's been great working with Bill," said the governor, "and I think it sends a strong message."[246]

Branstad has two offices in the Iowa State Capitol, one for official meetings and one for more private meetings. The latter is nicely furnished and adorned with photos that inspire him—from famous people to places he has visited. There are three photos of Abraham Lincoln on the wall and one of George Washington on his knees, in his general's uniform, praying at Valley Forge in the dead of a severe winter, when his hopes of winning the American Revolution were at the lowest ebb. The aforementioned "Tough Times" sign (that is the title of Robert Schuler's book) has been with him for nearly thirty years. "When we moved from the governor's office to Des Moines University and then back to the governor's office, that always went with us," said Margaret Hough. "It's very important to him."[247]

There is also a full-color photo of a huge elephant standing by a narrow dirt road in Africa, staring straight at the photographer, perhaps pondering if it would be a good moment to charge; it is a photo taken by Branstad himself. The photo opportunity came in 2007 when he was on a trip to South Africa with Dr. James Blessner, who spends several weeks each year in Linpopo Province providing free health care to the citizens.

"We saw rhinos, lions, elephants—it was an amazing trip," said the governor. "But what's more amazing is the work that Jim does there. I was along to give a lecture on medical ethics. I didn't know much about the subject but read a lot on the plane ride over. It was very interesting."[248]

There were the fun times, such as when Arnold Schwarzenegger visited the Iowa State Capitol at the governor's request to promote physical fitness ("That's the one time all my kids wanted to come to the office," said Branstad with a chuckle), or playing baseball with movie stars and former major league baseball players at the *Field of Dreams* movie site on August 2, 1991. (There was even a photo in one newspaper of Terry Branstad sliding into a base under the tag of actor D. B. Sweeney, who played Shoeless Joe Jackson in the 1988 hit movie.)

There were the trips to California to stand tall and proud on the deck of the USS *Iowa* during important occasions.

There were the numerous trips to Washington, DC, to hobnob with the nation's top leaders.

There was the occasion of standing with Iowa's Olympic wrestling legends in 2013 to announce that Iowa would stand against the decision of the International Olympic Committee to drop the sport from the games.

Rick Perry, governor of Texas, who has visited Iowa many times to campaign for the nomination for the presidency on the Republican ticket, has lauded Branstad for being an excellent salesman for the state, and hardly anyone would dispute that notion. He has been an indefatigable crusader, spreading his love for Iowa from border to border, year after year.

"He is an expert at remembering people he has met," said David Roederer, his 1990 campaign director and former chief of staff who moved on to become director of management for the state of Iowa. "It's like he has a photographic memory. We could be at an event and someone would bring up something that happened a long time ago, and he remembers. He remembers people and events, and that makes them relate so well to him. In this day and age, people are looking for more than just the silver tongue. He's in politics for all the right reasons."[249]

Of course, Branstad doesn't spend all his time with power players and other politicians. He loves to go to festivals, fairs, picnics, ribbon cuttings, and, most of all, schools.

"Welcomed by 300 students waving Old Glory, Terry Branstad was in his glory as he entered Grant Elementary School here," wrote Jonathan Roos of the *Des Moines Register* in 1990 about the governor's trip to Waterloo. "Although there was not an eligible voter among them, the governor shook as many small, outstretched hands as he could as he passed between two lines of flag-carrying students.

"The students serenaded him with the Iowa Waltz, and he gave a short speech on the value of education. They gave him a coffee cup, a T-shirt and an armful of crayon drawings. He visited virtually every classroom, posed for pictures and signed the cast on a girl's arm.

"It was the sort of visit Branstad has made many times in his eight years as Iowa's governor."

". . . Terry Branstad has all the makings of a traveling salesman. He loves people, never seems to tire of his work, never stops smiling, sets specific goals and is enthusiastic about his product."[250]

No less of an authority than Robert Ray once praised his successor's ability to connect with people: "Terry Branstad is a master politician. He's very, very good at it. He loves it and it shows." In the same article, Steffen Schmidt, an Iowa State political professor, called Branstad's "ability to work a crowd amazing."[251]

Branstad also has a strong religious faith and came by his Catholicism in a circuitous route. His mother was Jewish and his father Lutheran, but shortly after meeting Chris, he converted to Catholicism. He makes a strong effort to attend Mass whenever he can, and that includes when traveling.

"Terry is very pious," said Doug Gross. "We were flying to Japan shortly after John Paul II became pope, and Terry was telling me about all the work John Paul had done in Poland to stave off communism. He got emotional and tears were streaming down his face as he was telling me the stories."[252]

In the final analysis, one of the biggest factors in the remarkable career of Terry Branstad is a quality that helped make Ronald Reagan so successful. It's called likeability. "Terry Branstad is one of the nicest politicians you'll ever meet," wrote Dennis Ryerson, editor of the *Des Moines Register*, in a 1991 column. "He's absolutely sincere, the kind of guy you'd like to have along on a Saturday morning run, a person who would be a caring neighbor.

"He loves Iowa. He travels all over the state, from Hamburg to Lansing, Rock Rapids to Fort Madison. He's all but addicted to the community meetings and Rotary lunches and ribbon cuttings that are so much a part of a governor's duties."[253]

While the governor has a host of fans from the ranks of those who have worked for him, none are more enthusiastic than Bonnie Smalley, who served as his scheduler for seventeen years, from 1982 through 1999. It's a behind-the-scenes job that requires superb administrative and personal communication skills but has a high burnout rate due to long hours and extreme attention to detail. But Bonnie, who now works at Wellmark Blue Cross and Blue Shield in Des Moines, is unrestrained when talking about the experience. She first met Branstad when her husband, Doug, was in the Iowa House with him, and she was working for another legislator, Ing Hansen of O'Brien County.

Doug Smalley was among the small circle of supporters Branstad brought together for consultation when he first decided to run for governor. Branstad asked Bonnie Smalley if she would be his scheduler.

"I told him I would support him any way I could—stuff envelopes and make calls, things like that—but that I had no experience in being a scheduler," said Smalley in 2015. "But he was so persistent. He kept asking me, and I finally said I would do it. But I had a little girl at home, and before I accepted the position, I told him that family would always come first. He said 'absolutely,' and he never once asked anyone to do something that went against family. He's so family-oriented.

"It's not a glamorous job, and it has a high burnout rate," she said. "The normal scheduler lasts for about eighteen months. It's a thankless job in most respects, and it's fast and furious. Obviously you can't fulfill all the requests that come in, but the governor was so wonderful to work for. He is so understanding and such a hard worker himself.

"I scheduled for him during the 1982 campaign and didn't know what to expect. Whenever I felt sorry for myself, I looked at his schedule and thought, 'How does he do this?' It was just amazing to watch him in action.

"My desk was right by his private entrance, and it was the first thing he saw every morning when he arrived and the last thing he saw when he left for the day. He would stop at my desk and say, 'Well, maybe we didn't get much done today, but we'll give it heck tomorrow." And I would think—look at all you did today.

"I think it goes back to his farm upbringing," she said. "He was given an awful lot of responsibility at a young age. I'll tell you one thing for sure—no one on this planet will ever outwork Terry Branstad.

"Another thing—he prides himself at being on time. He values other people's time, and he will make every effort not to keep people waiting." She told of one visit early in his career when the Waterloo executive lining up the visit wanted to bet her that the governor would not arrive on time because no other politician he lined up had ever done so.

She told the Waterloo executive that being a government employee she could not take the bet, but if she could she would bet a thousand dollars Branstad would be on schedule. The man called her the day of the visit and said he wanted to send her a large box of chocolates because she was correct—Branstad not only showed up on time but he was even a little early.

"He has a memory like a steel trap and loves this state like no one else," said Smalley. "It was such a pleasure and an honor to have worked for him."[254]

So where does he rank among the state's best governors?

"Anyone who has underestimated Terry Branstad over time has done so to their own detriment," said Jeff Stein, who has a law degree and has taught communications at both Wartburg College and William Penn University and *covered Iowa politics and elections for newspapers, radio, and television outlets for thirty-five years.* "He may not have the natural charisma of some, or the stereotypical good looks of other politicians . . . but all he does is win.

"His work ethic and devotion to the state of Iowa are legendary. While he may not be looked upon as fondly as Robert Ray, that is as much a product of the times in which he served as anything else. Ray guided Iowa in the aftermath of the turbulent '60s, with an easy-going style and demeanor that won him allies across the political aisle. Succeeding Ray was no easy feat, but Branstad has set himself apart through not only longevity but in skillfully guiding the state through parts of three very different decades.

"Even his critics have to admit that while they may not agree with all the measures he has taken, he sincerely believes he is acting in the best interest of Iowa and its citizens. That explains his passion for various issues and reluctance to compromise when he feels his path is the correct one. Most Iowans would want their governor to be of firm conviction, and if that comes off as combative at times, then so be it . . . he believes in himself and his decisions.

"It is increasingly true in politics in our Internet/social media age that there are work horses and there are show horses—the latter is more concerned with creating snappy YouTube videos and sound bites for media cameras, while the former goes about his business and gets things done. Terry Branstad is a work horse, and Iowans have rewarded that trait with a tenure in office unmatched in U.S. history."[255]

In January 1999, just prior to leaving office for the first time and entering into private business, Governor Branstad was asked by the *Des Moines Register* to list his top accomplishments over his sixteen years of leadership. The governor stated that he hoped future generations would acknowledge first and foremost his efforts to restore the economy from the damage it had suffered during the farm crisis of the 1980s.

"That's the thing that I am most proud of . . . is having turned the Iowa economy around from being on the wrong track to being on the right track," he told Jonathan Roos of the *Des Moines Register.* Then he listed six other areas in which he felt pride.

Turning around Iowans' attitudes to believing the state is on the right track by creating jobs and opportunities;

Improving the state's management and fiscal condition, creating a financial surplus, and reforming budget practices;

His work in education, including statewide fiber-optic network connecting every school district by 1999, and other education initiatives;

Public safety work, getting rid of the cap on prison populations, building enough prisons to keep the most violent and dangerous criminals off the streets, and pushing for tougher drunk driving and juvenile justice laws;

Welfare reform rolls dropping 34 percent and focusing on helping people get education, training, and jobs;

Better protection of women and children, and ordering arrests in domestic abuse cases and improving children's health programs.

All were substantial efforts aided by the legislators on both sides of the aisles working with him, of course. During his first ten years in office, Democrats controlled both the Iowa House and Senate. Still, they "acknowledge that he has accomplished much of what he proposed to the legislature," wrote Roos. "One example was Branstad's drive to reorganize the state bureaucracy. 'We dealt him pretty wide discretion in that area back in '86 and did significantly consolidate power in the governor's office,' said (Senate Majority Leader Michael) Gronstal."[256]

For two decades he has shown how much he cares about Iowa and Iowans. There are plenty who don't like his policies and disagree with his decisions, but very few who would debate his sincere affection for Iowa. Along the way, he made tremendous sacrifices and rode into the history books.

And he has tried to make education a top priority throughout his long tenure, pushing for a huge education program on several occasions and earning the endorsement of the Iowa State Education Association in the 1990 race.

"I can remember him quoting his mother many times," said Tim Albrecht. "She used to tell him to get an education 'because that is something no one can ever take away from you.' The governor really believes that education is the key to a great state."[257]

Branstad also expressed considerable pleasure infor the renovation work at the Iowa State Capitol and Iowa State Fairgrounds. Because man-made structures are subject to the passage of time, both the exterior façades and load-bearing interiors erode as the years slip by. They periodically require refortifying and renewing, making these symbols of the past consistently viable while providing the necessary care that allows new generations to walk their halls and marvel at what once was. As a lover of history, Governor Branstad has always been committed to preserving beautiful and functional facilities whenever possible.

The Iowa State Capitol is *the* icon of governance of the state. More than just a building on a hill overlooking Des Moines, it represents both the country's westward expansion and the state's rich history—as well as housing the current governmental staffs and work areas.

The cornerstone of the Iowa State Capitol was laid on November 23, 1871. The original cost was not to exceed $1.5 million, but the final expenditures totaled $2,873,294.59 due to setbacks and additional funds approved by the legislature. After a fire in the north wing in 1904, repair, modernization, and projects originally unfunded during the building's construction were commissioned. With those expenditures included, the total rose to $3.3 million.

In 1913, the statehouse passed controversial legislation to acquire additional land surrounding the thirteen-acre capitol grounds. The prevailing argument was to expand the capitol complex area to eliminate the "shanties and shacks" directly bordering it. Opponents used political advertisements, such as the one on November 2, 1914, in the *Atlantic News-Telegraph*, to point out the capitol extension park would total 83.04 acres and thus be larger than the combined capitol grounds of seventeen states, including New York and Illinois. It was pointed out that those seventeen states totaled 81.160 acres.

During the 1920s and 1930s, a statehouse decorator, Joseph Szizek, made many interior changes. By the 1950s, the Victorian style of dark paint with elegant stenciling from the original décor had been covered by the contemporary standard, no-frills white or light-colored paint. Most of the restorations over the years focused on the interior of the building. In 1965, the dome was regilded and some efforts were made for preserving the exterior walls.

The celebration of the nation's bicentennial in 1976 ushered in a newfound ambition to return the capitol back to its original Victorian glory. Research, painting, intricate stenciling, and other meticulous interior design tasks undertaken by professionals lasted years. By the early 1980s, deterioration of the exterior of the Iowa State Capitol Building had become an eyesore in some places and a potential safety liability. Steel canopies had to be erected over all entrances because chunks of sandstone block were beginning to fall from the exterior. Ornate decorations had eroded beyond recognition because of decades of weather and improper drainage from the rooftops. The lack of reliable drainage caused seepage of water on both the exterior and interior walls of the structure, wreaking havoc on almost every surface, nook, and cranny.

The first stone was removed in 1983. When the last stone was set in 2000, nearly 95 percent of the ornamental and trim sandstone had been replaced—7,500 tons in all. Another round of interior updating occurred following a 1991 task force's recommendations for the following: installation of a sprinkler system; removing intermediate floors; replacing the existing mechanical system; installation of new electrical and communications systems; and the continuation of the historical accuracy updates for the interior renovation.

Governor Branstad lent his considerable support to all the work that took place during his tenure. He was also very supportive of the formation of a blue ribbon committee to provide leadership on the renovation of the Iowa State Fairgrounds.

With annual visitors usually totaling around a million people, the Iowa State Fair has been a staple on the calendar of many Iowans since 1854, making it one of the largest fair and agricultural and industrial expositions in the country. The 450-acre plot of land that encompasses "America's classic state fair" was first introduced in 1886. Since then, many renovations and modernization efforts have evolved and allowed the event to continue for generations.

In 1923, the Iowa Legislature created a separate Iowa State Fair Board to manage the event. Prior, the fair was under the management of the Iowa State Agricultural Society and a board of agriculture. The original members of the new state fair board consisted of the governor, secretary of agriculture, the president of the Iowa State Agricultural College (Iowa State University), and one elected director from each of the six congressional districts, and three at-large directors, in addition to a secretary/manager and treasurer elected by the board.

In 1983, Governor Branstad, working with the Iowa Beef Industry and the Iowa Cattleman's Association, started the annual Governor's Charity Steer Show. All proceeds are donated to the Ronald McDonald Houses of Iowa in Des Moines, Iowa City, and Sioux City. These facilities support families with critically ill children, providing them with a "home away from home" while their children are being treated at a nearby hospital. The donations assist with the cost of staying at the houses. By the end of the fair in 2014, the event had raised over $2.5 million since 1983. In 2014, records were broken for a third consecutive year, with the show raising over $225,000. And for the thirtieth straight year, Terry Branstad was one of those showing a steer, while Lt. Governor Kim Reynolds showed the grand champion.

"It's one of the things I really enjoy doing, and the cause is great," said the governor. "The state fair is such a part of our state's heritage, and I'm proud to help in any way I can."[258]

It appears that Terry Branstad himself has become an integral part of the state's heritage. The case can be made that he has had a larger impact on the state than any other single individual, and if it's true that you can tell the most about a man from the people who worked for him, then Branstad's legacy is secure.

Insiders say there is no more demanding job in all of state politics than chief of staff of a governor, with its myriad pressures and demands. In the words of one reporter, it's a brutal job with a high burnout rate. On August 30, 2013, Jeff Boeynik announced that he was stepping down as Branstad's chief of staff and entering private business. After running the successful 2010 campaign, he headed up the transition team and then went straight into the chief of staff position. He said he was looking forward to taking his first vacation since 2008.

And then he offered a statement that sums up the feelings of many people who have stood alongside America's longest serving governor: "Working for Terry Branstad has been the biggest honor of my life," he said, "and the decision to leave this office is the most difficult I have ever made."[259]

What has impressed Kim Reynolds the most in her time as lieutenant governor is what all those who came before her have discovered: "His love for the state of Iowa is immeasurable. The schedule he keeps and the way he and Chris inspire everyone is remarkable. Everyone is so comfortable around him; I think that's one of the real keys to his success. I'm just so proud to be a part of the team."[260]

Dating all the way back to his formative years in tiny Leland and to the present day, Terry Branstad has left a mark on those who came in contact with him with his energy, enthusiasm, passion, and work ethic. It's a legacy that is bound to endure for generations to come.

CHAPTER FOURTEEN

History of Iowa Governors

Terry Branstad occupies a very special position in the long history of Iowa governors, being the youngest to ever hold office (age thirty-six), winning the most elections (six), being one of just two men to leave the office and then return (Samuel Kirkwood is the other), and being the longest serving governor ever.

However, there are some other amazing stories among the forty-one men who have served as governor of the state of Iowa. They have come from various walks of life with surprising backgrounds—several fought in the Civil War, one was a brigadier general, another was governor of Ohio before moving to Iowa, one was a stagecoach driver, and yet another was grandfather of the greatest football star in Iowa history!

The land that would become known as Iowa became part of the United States of America in 1803 when President Thomas Jefferson signed the deal for the Louisiana Purchase. By acquiring this immense piece of land—nearly 828,000 square miles—from France for a cost of approximately $15 million, Jefferson was able to double the size of the nation . . . at about four cents an acre, or just 42 cents an acre in 2014 money.

What is now called Iowa was included in the Missouri Territory until 1821 and then became part of Michigan Territory until 1836, when it was absorbed into the Wisconsin Territory. For ten years, from 1836 to 1846, it was simply called the Iowa Territory. On December 30, 1846, it was admitted into the Union as the twenty-ninth state.

As the nation continued its westward expansion in the early 1800s, hardy men and women crossed the Mississippi River and began moving farther into what would become Iowa at a rapid pace, encouraged by stories of the rolling prairie that could support crops like wheat and corn. The promise of a new life on the frontier was appealing to many, but it was also a decision that brought with it a staunch commitment to hard work and long hours of toil. The land was heavily dotted with thick pockets of forest, and the tough task of clearing trees and plowing the ground, along with the threat of Indian attacks and the prospect of enduring severe winters, was enough to discourage all but the most determined.

The arrival of large groups of settlers into the Iowa Territory soon demanded structure and rules and someone to steer the ship of state. The role of government in the 1840s was to make certain there was an orderly degree of transition from the primitive state to an organized society that would protect citizens and their rights and enforce laws. A governor has many responsibilities, foremost of which is to serve as the executive officer of the state government, and also to be commander in chief of the state's military. He or she has the authority to enforce state laws and to either approve or veto bills that are passed by the state legislature, which includes both the house and the senate.

Besides those primary duties, the governor has the power to call the legislature into session at any time, and he or she can also grant pardons and reprieves in cases that don't involve treason or impeachment.

When the position was first authorized, it was for a two-year term, but in 1972 a constitutional amendment was passed making it a four-year term. A person wishing to run for the highest office in the state must be at least thirty years old at the time of taking office and must have been an Iowa citizen for two full years.

The first official governor of the Iowa Territory was Ansell Briggs, who served from 1846 to 1850, and to date the position has been dominated by Republicans. Of the forty-one different men who have been governor, thirty were from the Republican Party, ten were Democrats, and one was a member of the now defunct Whig Party.

Four other men actually served as territorial governors before Iowa became a state, but one was merely an acting territorial governor for six weeks. William B. Conway was born in Delaware in 1802 and was a lawyer in Pittsburgh, Pennsylvania, in the spring of 1838 when President Martin Van Buren appointed him acting governor of Iowa until Robert Lucas could be sworn in as territorial governor. So technically, the honor of being Iowa's first governor goes to this young man from Delaware.

It was reported that Conway and Lucas did not have a high regard for each other, and when Lucas took over the post, they had an acrimonious relationship. Lucas proved to be rather difficult for others he came in contact with during the three years he held the position, to the point where President Van Buren and the US Congress decided to limit his powers to vetoing and making appointments.

Before arriving in Iowa, Lucas had an extraordinary background. He was born in 1781 in Virginia, along the Potomac River, where George Washington grew to manhood. His father fought in the Revolutionary War, and Robert moved to the Ohio Territory around age twenty. He began a military career and wound up a brigadier general, serving in the War of 1812. He began a career in politics and eventually became speaker of the Ohio State Senate.

Lucas was elected governor of Ohio in 1832 and after serving his term decided to move west, across the Mississippi River, into the Iowa portion of the Wisconsin Territory. In 1837, the territorial capital was located in Burlington, but two years later the legislature voted to move it to Iowa City. However, Iowa City did not officially become the acting capital until 1841.

Lucas was governor from 1838 to 1841, moving to Iowa City at the end of his term. He and his wife, Friendly, built a beautiful home there, which is now owned by the state and is open to the public much of the year. It is called the Plum Grove Historic Site and is situated on Kirkwood Avenue, which is named for the fifth governor of Iowa. Lucas died in 1853 at the age of seventy-one and is buried in Iowa City.

Next in line was John Chambers, a native of New Jersey who had been a member of Congress while residing in Kentucky. A lawyer by trade, he also served in the War of 1812 and was Iowa territorial governor from 1841 to 1845. A member of the Whig Party, he died in 1852, also at the age of seventy-one.

The third territorial governor was James Clarke, a native of Pennsylvania who wound up as mayor of Burlington. He was a printer and publisher by trade and had served as a territorial secretary under Governor Lucas. Clarke was appointed territorial governor by President James Polk on November 8, 1845, four years after the capital was moved from Burlington to Iowa City.

Clarke was involved with establishing Iowa's boundaries and helped lay the foundation for Iowa's admission into the Union, which took place shortly after he retired as governor. He returned home to Burlington to run the newspaper he had founded there and met a tragic end. A cholera epidemic struck Burlington with a vengeance, first killing his wife and infant son, and then Clarke, at age thirty-eight.

It was Ansel Briggs who provided the bridge between the two types of governors—the men who led the territorial system and those who sat at the head of the official state government. Born in 1816 in Vermont, Briggs moved west with his family as a young boy. He came to the Iowa Territory in 1839 to run a stagecoach business and often drove the routes from Dubuque, Davenport, and Iowa City himself.

Briggs and his wife, Nancy, first settled in Jackson County, named for President Andrew Jackson, and then moved to the village of Andrew, where they began acquiring land. Originally a Whig, he switched to the Democratic Party and on October 28, 1846, defeated a Whig opponent, Thomas McKnight, to become the first official governor of Iowa. He was a no-nonsense sort of administrator who helped develop the governmental system and the school structure for the state. He served two terms and moved to Council Bluffs in 1870, twenty years after retiring as governor. He died in 1881 and is buried in the Andrew Cemetery.

Stephen P. Hempstead was born in Connecticut in 1812 and came to Iowa as a young man. A Democrat, he served in the territorial legislature and was elected governor in 1850, where he helped to write laws that became the foundation of the Iowa Code. He served four years, from 1850 to 1854, then returned to Dubuque and was a judge before dying in 1883. He is buried in Dubuque, where a public high school is named for him.

He was followed by James W. Grimes, an attorney from Burlington (born in New Hampshire), who served from 1854 to 1858. According to Richard Doak, a retired editorial page editor of the *Des Moines Register* who is a lecturer at Iowa State University and an adjunct instructor at Simpson College, Grimes is one of the six greatest governors in state history.

"Grimes' election in 1854 sparked a political revolution in Iowa and much of the North," wrote Doak. "His Whig Party joined with disaffected Democrats and remnants of the Know Nothing Party to create a new Republican Party that would dominate Iowa for seventy years."[261]

He presided over many aspects of the government still in effect today, including the move of the capital from Iowa City to Des Moines and the drafting of a new state constitution. After his governor days were over, he was elected to the United States Senate and was one of seven Republicans senators who broke ranks and voted against the impeachment of President Andrew Johnson, thereby saving Johnson from the dishonor of being removed from office.

The city of Grimes is named in his honor, and an elementary school bearing his name sits on the ground where his home once stood. He died in 1872 at age fifty-five and is buried in Burlington.

On January 13, 1858, Ralph P. Lowe took over the governor's office, and the GOP held onto it for the next thirty-two years. Born in Ohio, Lowe moved to Muscatine and was working as a judge when he won the governorship in a tight race. He served just one term and then spent several years on the Iowa Supreme Court before moving to Washington, DC, where he died and is buried.

Iowa's fourth governor, Samuel J. Kirkwood, played a prominent role in the Civil War, serving as a supporter of Abraham Lincoln during his presidency. Also ranked as one of the six top governors by Doak, he helped build a pride among Iowans that has endured ever since.

Born in 1813 in Maryland, Kirkwood was a school teacher early in life and moved to Ohio in 1835. He developed an intense dislike for slavery. He moved to Iowa, near Iowa City, in 1855 and became heavily involved in Republican politics. He was elected to the Iowa

Senate in 1856 and became governor in 1860 after a heated battle that centered on slavery.

In 1861, Kirkwood traveled to Springfield, Illinois, to confer with Lincoln before he departed for Washington, DC, to take over as the nation's sixteenth president. When the South attacked Fort Sumter on April 12, 1861, Lincoln issued a proclamation calling for seventy-five thousand troops to suppress the uprising. The Civil War had begun!

According to William C. Harris in the book *Lincoln and the Union Governors*, Kirkwood "received news of Lincoln's proclamation while caring for his livestock" and "indicated that fifteen to twenty volunteer companies had been immediately raised for the army. The Iowa governor even moved his office to Davenport, at the end of the telegraph line, where he would have immediate contact with Lincoln and the War Department. Like most Northern governors, Kirkwood spoke at mass rallies supporting the war and encouraging volunteering in the state units."[262]

In 1863, the Union states were being hammered by war dissent and urgently requested more supplies and equipment. Kirkwood wrote to Lincoln that he feared the prospect of a disaster in Iowa "if the War Department did not supply him with the necessary arms for his militia or home guard."[263]

At one point, Harris reports that "Governor Kirkwood actually extended his personal credit to help clothe three Iowa regiments, only to be bluntly notified by his bankers when the notes fell due. In other states, some banks were more supportive and some even paid for the arms outright."[264]

Kirkwood also charged that a group known as Knights of the Golden Circle was working the state, calling for desertions by Iowa soldiers in the army and mass protests at home. He thought there was a chance of armed resistance that could result in a civil war in Iowa. Though it never happened, Kirkwood was alarmed and said so.

According to Harris, Kirkwood was one of the most outspoken governors when it came to using black troops in the war. Kirkwood declared that if black people were "willing to pay for their freedom by fighting for those who make them free, I am entirely willing that they should do so."[265]

Kirkwood did not run for reelection in the fall of 1863, and William M. Stone became Iowa's new governor in January 1864. He was also a backer of Lincoln, but more reserved in his support than some of the other governors of the North.

Stone is one of the fascinating figures in Iowa history, but remains little known. Born in New York, he moved to Knoxville, Iowa, in 1854, where he operated a law practice and owned the local newspaper. He later served as a state district court judge.

When the Civil War broke out, Stone enlisted as a private and rose steadily through the ranks, and served gallantly in several major battles. In 1862, he was promoted to colonel of the Twenty-Second Iowa Infantry and led the Iowans into the Battle of Vicksburg, where he was wounded. Stone left the army in the summer of 1863 and ran for Iowa governor, winning by a large margin.

Feeling Lincoln could not win reelection in 1864, some top-level Republicans wanted Lincoln replaced on the ticket with another candidate for president. Asked for his assessment of Lincoln's chances to win again, Governor Stone wrote, "Running on his own merit or personal popularity, Lincoln could not win." But, Stone added, "The voters understood 'the mighty issue at stake' and 'the disastrous consequences which would inevitably result from his defeat.'"[266]

It wasn't a strong endorsement, but it was enough to help Lincoln carry the state of Iowa a second time. In fact, Lincoln won by a landslide in 1864, with an estimated 78 percent of Union soldiers voting for him. Five days after General Robert E. Lee surrendered the South, on April 9, 1865, Lincoln was shot and killed while attending a play in Ford's Theater. Iowa Governor Stone was one of the men who carried the mortally wounded president from the theater to the boarding house across the street, where he died the next morning.

Stone was reelected as Iowa governor in 1865, then served one term in the legislature. He moved to the Oklahoma Territory and died in 1893, at age sixty-two. He is buried in Graceland Cemetery in Knoxville.

While Stone was serving as governor, Kirkwood was also staying busy. He practiced law in Iowa City then moved on to the US Senate. In 1876, Kirkwood set a precedent that only one other Iowa governor would follow. After several years out of office, he ran for governor again, and won handily. Some 142 years later, Terry Branstad did the same, winning a fifth term after being out of office for twelve years.

Kirkwood resigned the governorship in 1877 to run for the senate again, and later became secretary of the interior under President James Garfield. He died in 1894 at age eighty and is buried in Iowa City. The large community college located in Cedar Rapids is named in his honor, as are streets in several cities. Doak, in rating Kirkwood as one of the best governors, said: "His singular achievement was to help forge an identity and self-image for Iowa. Indeed, Iowa was different after the war. There was a pride about being Iowans. The state took seriously its role in promoting human freedom."[267]

Samuel Merrill, a native of Maine, was the seventh Iowa governor, serving two terms with little distinction. After serving in the state legislature in New Hampshire, he moved to McGregor, Iowa, in 1856 and was elected to the Iowa Legislature. Merrill fought in the Civil War as a commissioned officer and suffered a hip wound that plagued him the rest of his life. He served as governor from 1868 to 1872 and is buried in Des Moines.

He was followed by Cyrus C. Carpenter, a Pennsylvanian who moved to the Fort Dodge area in 1854, working as a surveyor. He was elected to the Iowa House in 1858, volunteered for service in the Civil War, and reached the rank of colonel. He won two terms as governor, from 1872 to 1876, and then was elected to the US Congress. He returned to the Iowa House for two more years and died in 1898. He is buried in Fort Dodge.

Carpenter was followed by Kirkwood in his abbreviated second stint as governor. The Republican string was continued by Joshua G. Newbold, who grew up as a Quaker in Pennsylvania and came to Iowa at age twenty-four, in 1854, to farm. He joined the Twenty-Fifth Regiment of the Iowa Infantry as a captain and saw extensive action in major battles of the Civil War. He was elected to the Iowa House of Representatives in 1872, then became lieutenant governor in 1876, and took over for Kirkwood when he resigned to become a US senator. Newbold served for nearly a year, and then moved to Mount Pleasant, where he was elected mayor. He died in 1903, at age seventy-two.

A native of New York, John Gear moved to Burlington, Iowa, in 1843, and was elected mayor twenty years later. He served in the Iowa House from 1871 to 1877, and was elected governor in 1878, then became a US congressman and senator. He died in 1900, at the age of seventy-five, and is buried in Burlington.

Iowa's twelfth governor was Buren R. Sherman, also from New York. A lawyer, he moved to Vinton, Iowa, in 1855 and enlisted to fight in the Civil War, reaching the rank of captain before being injured at the Battle of Shiloh. He was governor from 1882 to 1886, and died in 1904. He is buried in Vinton.

William Larrabee grew up on the family farm in Connecticut and moved to Iowa at the age of twenty-one, pursuing careers in teaching and banking in Clermont. He became a huge landowner and was one of the organizers of the new and powerful Republican Party in Iowa. He was elected to the state senate in 1867, and became governor for two terms, serving from1886 to 1890. Larrabee died at age eighty in 1912, and is buried in Clermont. The family mansion, called Montauk, is still standing.

Horace Boies, a Democrat from New York who settled in Waterloo and became a lawyer, snapped the long string of Republican governors when he was elected to the office and took over in February 1890. Though originally a Republican, he switched parties when Republicans supported Prohibition and high tariffs. He served two terms and lived to be ninety-five, dying in 1923. He holds the distinction of being the only Democrat to serve as governor in a seventy-eight-year period, from 1855 to 1933.

Frank D. Jackson, Leslie M. Shaw, Albert Cummins, and Warren Garst were the next governors, Garst taking over after Cummings was elected to the US Senate. A year later, Garst lost in his own bid to become governor, and on January 14, 1909, Beryl F. Carroll made history by becoming the first native Iowan to run the state. Born in

Davis County, he worked as a teacher, livestock leader, and newspaper publisher before entering politics. Carroll served two terms as Iowa's twentieth governor, from 1909 to 1913. He died in 1939 at age seventy-nine and is buried in Bloomfield, Iowa.

A bank robbery in Adel on March 6, 1895, nearly cost Iowa its twenty-first governor and the state its greatest football legend. On that day, two thugs entered the Adel Savings Bank and demanded money. A shot was fired, and George W. Clarke, a young attorney who was renting an office above the bank, ran down the stairs to see what was going on. One of the robbers pointed the gun at him and pulled the trigger, but the gun misfired and the thief ran from the bank.

Clarke went on to a long political career, first as a state legislator then as lieutenant governor, and finally as governor from 1912 to 1916. He was dean of the Drake Law School in 1917 and 1918, then practiced law in Des Moines. Clarke died in 1936 at the age of eighty-four. His grandson, Nile Clarke Kinnick, won the Heisman Trophy for the University of Iowa in 1939 and was named Associated Press Male Athlete of the Year. The Iowa football stadium was named for Kinnick in 1972.

Today, a bust of Governor Clarke sits in the office of Terry Branstad. Not only did Terry follow in Clarke's footsteps politically, but he earned his law degree at the school where Clarke served as dean.

The four years that William L. Harding spent in office were marked by several surprising actions on behalf of the twenty-second governor. A native of Sibley, Iowa, Harding was also an attorney and served in the state house and as lieutenant governor prior to winning two terms as governor. According to various accounts, "Harding opposed voting rights for women and road improvements. One of his most infamous acts was to issue the Babel Proclamation in 1918. This act, which is widely believed to be unconstitutional, forbade the use of foreign languages in public, over the telephone, in school, and in religious services. It came about due to the large anti-German sentiment during the First World War. His time in office was marred by other scandals. His hostility towards immigrant and other foreign ethnic groups extended beyond Germans and, for example, included Iowans of Norwegian descent."[268] Harding died at age fifty-seven and is buried in Sioux City.

Three more Republicans—Nathan E. Kendall (1921–1925), John Hammill (1925–1931), and Daniel Webster Turner—held the office until the Democrats finally put one of their own back in the leadership role of the state. Clyde H. Herring was born in Michigan and lived in Colorado before moving to Massena, Iowa, in 1906 and taking up farming. He became an agent for the Ford car company and purchased extensive real estate in Des Moines.

Herring lost early bids for governor and the US Senate, but he defeated incumbent Daniel Webster Turner and assumed the governor's chair for two terms, from 1932 to 1936. Doak picked him as one of the six greatest governors, saying that beyond his crisis management during the Great Depression, "his most lasting contribution was in remaking state government itself. This was done by reorganizing the state's budget and enacting the three taxes that are the mainstays of state government today—sales, income and corporation taxes. These taxes had not existed in Iowa before. They enabled the state to assume many of the burdens previously carried by counties and local schools through property taxes. It is impossible to imagine a modern state government functioning today without the taxes enacted during Herring's tenure as governor."[269]

Herring left the governor's office and won election as a US senator and had hopes of being Franklin D. Roosevelt's vice-presidential nominee in 1940, but fellow Iowan Henry Wallace was picked instead. Herring died in 1945 at the age of sixty-six and is buried in Des Moines.

Republicans were back in control, with six more in a row, starting with George A. Wilson (1939–1943). Following in order were Bourke B. Hickenlooper (1943–1945), Robert D. Blue (1945–1949), William S. Beardsley (1949–1954), Leo Elthon (1954–1955), and Leo A. Hoegh (1955–1957).

Herschel C. Loveless carried the Democratic banner for two terms, 1957 to 1961, but Norman E. Erbe put the Republicans back on top, from 1961 to 1963. Erbe's reelection effort set the stage for one of the most intriguing political contests in state history and opened the door for one of the most charismatic governors ever.

A native of Boone, Erbe had been an infantry officer and pilot during World War II, then earned a law degree from Iowa. He served as attorney general and then became Iowa's thirty-fifth governor in 1961. Running for a second term, he came face to face with Harold Hughes—a former all-state football player, truck driver, World War II soldier, and recovering alcoholic.

Born and raised in Ida Grove in northwestern Iowa, Hughes grew up a Republican but switched parties and defeated Erbe in a hotly contested battle. Hughes was a very popular figure and won re-election easily in 1966, then ran for the US Senate and grabbed that seat, serving from 1969 to 1975. A born-again Christian, Hughes turned his back on politics to concentrate on helping recovering alcoholics and espousing the Christian lifestyle.

Hughes made Doak's list of the top six governors: "In his second term, Hughes had an overwhelmingly Democratic legislature produced by the Democratic landslide of 1964, and he led a historically productive session in 1965. Among other things, that session abolished capital punishment, created the system of area community colleges and enacted civil rights legislation."[270]

Of course, the "Democratic landslide" came about when Lyndon Johnson, the incumbent president, crushed challenger Barry Goldwater, the author of the conservative movement that had inspired so many Republicans, including a young Forest City student named Terry Branstad.

Though he strongly considered running for governor again in 1981 and had the backing of Bill Knapp, the top Democratic fundraiser in the state, Hughes opted not to run when a problem arose over his eligibility on the requirement that all candidates had to reside in the state two years prior. Hughes had been living in DC, and he decided not to challenge a ruling by the secretary of state that he would not be eligible.[271]

That decision would not only affect politics at the time, but would leave Samuel Kirkwood and Terry Branstad alone on the list of men who had won the governorship after leaving office.

When Hughes left Iowa to take his senate seat in 1969, Robert D. Fulton, his lieutenant governor, became the thirty-seventh governor of the state. A native of Waterloo, Fulton had previously served in the Iowa House and Senate before becoming Hughes's second in command. He held the governor's chair for just sixteen days in January 1969. Hughes retired to private life and died at age seventy-four in Glendale, Arizona.

Following the popular Democrat Harold Hughes was a Republican destined to become every bit as popular, and who held the record for longevity in the office, until it was broken by his former lieutenant governor.

Robert Ray didn't have far to travel to become governor. He was born in Des Moines on September 26, 1928, graduated from Roosevelt High School, and received a BA in business from Drake University in 1952. He received his law degree from Drake in 1954. He entered into private practice but soon found his way into politics, serving as chair of the Iowa Republican Party. Faced with the monumental task of helping rebuild the party after a devastating defeat in 1964 suffered by Barry Goldwater in the presidential race, Ray proved up to the task. In November 1968, he was elected governor and held that office for a total of twelve years—from January 16, 1969, until January 14, 1983.

He was a dynamic leader who made significant improvements in many areas of Iowa life. He was elected chair of the National Governors Association in 1975 and held a number of top positions within the Republican leadership. He was an advocate for improving the status of women and children, and promoted civil rights and government ethics.

During his first term, the governor's length of office was changed from two to four years, and in 1976, he and his wife, Billie, became the first couple to live at Terrace Hill. One of his most memorable acts was to champion the cause of Southeast Asian refugees to come to the United State and eventually gain citizenship. In 2005, Ray became the only former Iowa governor to receive the Iowa Award, which is regarded as the highest civilian honor in the state, given by the Iowa Centennial Memorial Commission.

After leaving office, he became CEO of Life Investors, then president and CEO of Blue Cross and Blue Shield of Iowa, and later president of Drake University. One of his pet projects is the Keep Iowa Beautiful program, which has worked hard to make the state clean and beautiful for Iowans to enjoy. As a tribute to his many contributions and accomplishments, one of the main streets near the capitol is named Robert D. Ray Drive.

Ray was followed in the state's top office by young Terry Branstad, and the Leland native held that job for the next sixteen years before deciding to step aside. Many political insiders felt that Ross Lightfoot, a former US congressman, would continue the Republican monopoly on the governor's office. But that was not the case.

Tom Vilsack travelled an unlikely route to the governor's mansion. Born in Pittsburgh, Pennsylvania, he was placed in a Roman Catholic orphanage as a baby and was adopted in 1951 by Bud and Dolly Vilsack. While attending Hamilton College in New York, he met Ann Christine Bell of Mount Pleasant, Iowa, and they eventually married. He received his degree in 1972 and then his law degree from Albany Law School. In 1975, Tom and Christine Vilsack moved to Mount Pleasant, where he went to work in her father's law firm.

In 1987, Vilsack became mayor of Mount Pleasant, and five years later he was elected to the Iowa Senate. He won the Democratic nomination for governor and came from behind in the polls to defeat Lightfoot and become the first Democratic governor in thirty years, and only the fifth in the twentieth century. He won a second term in 2002 by defeating Republican challenger Doug Gross.

After serving two terms, Vilsack made a run for the Democratic nomination for president but dropped out after three months due to lack of funding. On January 21, 2009, he became the nation's thirtieth secretary of agriculture, appointed by President Obama.

His successor as governor was Chet Culver, another Democrat. The son of United States Senator John Culver, Chet was born and raised in Washington, DC. He attended Virginia Tech University on a football scholarship and graduated in 1988 with a degree in political science. He moved to Des Moines and earned a master's degree in education from Drake. He quickly moved into the political sphere and was selected secretary of state in 1998 and held the office for eight years.

When he decided to run for governor, Culver faced a three-person primary and won with 39 percent of the vote. He selected Patty Judge as his running mate. On January 27, 2007, Culver became the state's forty-first governor when he defeated Republican Jim Nussel, a former US congressman, by a 54–44 margin.

Four year later, in a matchup of current and past governors, Culver lost by a 52–43 margin to Terry Branstad, putting Republicans back in the governor's mansion after a twelve-year hiatus. In 2016, Branstad won easily over Democratic challenger Jack Hatch to further cement his legacy as Iowa's longest serving governor . . . and as America's longest serving governor as well.

Governors of Iowa – Territorial

1. Robert Lucas (Democrat) 1838–1841
2. John Chambers (Whig) 1841–1845
3. James Clarke (Democrat) 1845–1846

* *William B. Conway served briefly as acting governor in 1838 prior to Lucas taking over.*

Governors of Iowa - Official State

1. Ansel Briggs (Democrat) 1846–1850
2. Stephen P. Hempstead (Democrat) 1850–1854
3. James W. Grimes (Whig) 1854–1858
4. Ralph P. Lowe Republican) 1858–1860
5. Samuel J. Kirkwood (Republican) 1860–1864
6. William M. Stone (Republican) 1864–1868
7. Samuel Merrill (Republican) 1868–1872
8. Cyrus C. Carpenter (Republican) 1872–1876
9. Samuel J. Kirkwood (Republican) 1876–1877
10. Joshua G. Newbold (Republican) 1877–1878
11. John H. Gear (Republican) 1878–1882
12. Buren R. Sherman (Republican) 1882–1886
13. William Larrabee (Republican) 1886–1890
14. Horace Boies (Democrat) 1890–1894
15. Frank D. Jackson (Republican) 1894–1896
16. Francis M. Drake (Republican) 1896–1898
17. Leslie M. Shaw (Republican) 1898–1902
18. Albert M. Cummins (Republican) 1902–1908
19. Warren Garst (Republican) 1908–1909
20. Beryl F. Carroll (Republican) 1909–1913
21. George C. Clarke (Republican) 1913–1917
22. William L. Harding (Republican) 1917–1921
23. Nathan E. Kendall (Republican) 1921–1925
24. John Hammill (Republican) 1925–1931
25. Daniel Webster Turner (Republican) 1931–1933
26. Clyde L. Herring (Democrat) 1933–1937
27. Nelson G. Kraschel (Democrat) 1937–1939
28. George A. Wilson (Republican) 1939–1943
29. Bourke B. Hickenlooper (Republican) 1943–1945

30. Robert D. Blue (Republican) 1945–1949
31. William S. Beardsley (Republican) 1949–1954
32. Leo Elthon (Republican) 1954–1955
33. Leo A. Hoegh (Republican) 1955–1957
34. Herschel C. Loveless (Democrat) 1957–1961
35. Norman A. Erbe (Republican) 1961–1963
36. Harold E. Hughes (Democrat) 1963–1969
37. Robert D. Fulton (Democrat) 1969–1969
38. Robert D. Ray (Republican) 1969–1983
39. Terry E. Branstad (Republican) 1983–1999
40. Tom Vilsack (Democrat) 1999–2007
41. Chet Culver (Democrat) 2007–2011
42. Terry E. Branstad (Republican) 2011–current)

Longest Serving U.S. Governors

The following is a list of the nation's top 10 longest serving governors as compiled by Dr. Eric Ostermeier of the website smart politics. It does not include governors who served prior to the formation of the U.S. Constitution and thus does not show George Clinton, as many of his years in office were under the articles of confederation before the U.S. Constitution was ratified.

1. Terry Branstad, Iowa, Republican - 7,303 days (as of January 9, 2015)
2. Bill Janklow, South Dakota, Republican - 5,851 days
3. George Wallace, Alabama, Democrat – 5,848 days
4. Jim Rhodes, Ohio, Republican – 5,840 days
5. Jim Hunt, North Carolina, Democrat – 5,840 days
6. Edwin Edwards, Louisiana, Democrat– 5,784 days
7. Arthur Fenner, Rhode Island, Anti-Federalist – 5,642 days
8. Albert Ritchie, Maryland, Democrat – 5,475 days
9. Nelson Rockefeller, New York, Republican – 5,466 days
10. Rick Perry, Texas, Republican – 5,144 days

Terry Branstad's perfect 20–0 electoral record

1972 Iowa House District 8 Primary Election
Terry Branstad – R 1,668

1972 Iowa House District 8 General Election
Terry Branstad – R 7,368
Elmer Leibrand – D 5,130

1974 Iowa House District 8 Primary Election
Terry Branstad – R 1,189

1974 Iowa House District 8 General Election
Terry Branstad – R 6,699
Jean Haugland – D 3,046

1976 Iowa House District 8 Primary Election
Terry Branstad – R 1,742

1976 Iowa House District 8 General Election
Terry Branstad – R 8,553
Franklin Banwart – D 3,600

1978 Iowa Lt. Governor Primary Election
Terry Branstad – R 61,078
Willard Hansen – R 47,427
Brice Oakley – R 36,565

1978 Iowa Lt. Governor General Election
Terry Branstad – R 451,928
William Palmer – D 330,817

1982 Iowa Gubernatorial Primary Election
Terry Branstad – R 128,314

1982 Iowa Gubernatorial General Election
Terry Branstad – R 548,313
Roxanne Conlin – D 483, 291

1986 Iowa Gubernatorial Primary Election
Terry Branstad – R 104,482

1986 Iowa Gubernatorial General Election
Terry Branstad – R 472,712
Lowell Junkins – D 436,987

1990 Iowa Gubernatorial Primary Election
Terry Branstad – R 94,253

1990 Iowa General Election Governor
Terry Branstad – R 591,852
Don Avenson – D 379,372

1994 Iowa Primary for Governor
Terry Branstad – R 161,228
Fred Grandy – R 149,809

1994 Iowa General Election for Governor
Terry Branstad – R 566,395
Bonnie Campbell – D 414,453

2010 Iowa Primary Election for Governor
Terry Branstad – R 114,450
Bob Vander Plaats – R 93,058
Rod Roberts – R 19,896

2010 Iowa General Election for Governor
Terry Branstad – R 592,494
Chet Culver – D 484,798

2014 Iowa Primary Election for Governor
Terry Branstad – R 129,752
Tom Hoefling – D 26,299

2014 Iowa General Election for Governor
Terry Branstad – R 666,023
Jack Hatch – D 420,778

THE BRANSTAD FAMILY

Terry Edward Branstad: Born November 17, 1946, Forest City, Iowa
Christine (Johnson) Branstad: Born April 8, 1952, Fort Dodge, Iowa
Date Married: June 17, 1972
Children: Eric, Allison, Marcus

Eric Branstad
Born July 8, 1975
Spouse: Adrianne
Date Married: October 1, 2005
Children: Mackenzie, Bridget, Alexis

Allison Branstad Costa
Born: May 29, 1977
Spouse: Jerry Costa
Date Married: August 13, 2005
Children: Sofia, Estelle

Marcus Branstad
Born: January 22, 1984
Spouse: Nicole
Date Married: May 28, 2011
Child: Everett

Terry Branstad's Personal Observations

The Ingredients of Success

1. Positive Attitude

People with a positive attitude are fun to be around. They are enthusiastic and look for new opportunities with every setback. Some of the world's most successful leaders faced much adversity and numerous defeats, yet they were able to overcome and succeed as well as inspire others to follow their lead. Two great examples are Abraham Lincoln and Winston Churchill. Each of them was called on to lead his nation during some of the darkest and most difficult times of its history.

2. Set Ambitious Goals

Leaders are people with a clear vision of what they want to accomplish. They set goals to achieve their vision and measure their progress. To be successful, leaders must have the confidence of the people they lead, and that can be obtained by clearly communicating the goals, repeating them often, and demonstrating progress to achieve them.

3. Hard Work

I learned at an early age growing up on a farm to work hard. If any task is worth doing, it's worth doing well. Really successful people put in extraordinary amounts of time and effort to accomplish each assignment very well. This is true for athletes, entrepreneurs, musicians, and elected officials. It's also important as a leader that people know you care about them, their families, and the communities. In Iowa, as a state-elected official, a great way for me to demonstrate this is by visiting all ninety-nine counties every year.

4. Look for Opportunities

There is a human tendency to become comfortable doing things the way they have always been done. The really successful people are always looking for a simpler, safer, faster, more effective way to do things. That search for a better way has led to great inventions that have saved lives and improved the quality of life for countless people. Leaders always try to surround themselves with idea people, problem solvers, and risk takers who are constantly looking for a better way to accomplish the task.

5. Adjust to Changing Circumstances

If at first you don't succeed, try and try again. Learn from your mistakes and make changes and adjustments so that your proposal becomes more attractive to those who have constructively criticized it. Remember, most great inventions succeeded after many failures. Always look for opportunities to adjust your proposal to make a win-win for all parties involved.

6. Give Back

Be generous and give credit to all who help you. Successful people give generously of their personal resources to encourage and help others. Establishing scholarships and awarding grants to help future leaders and good causes are common characteristics of the most successful people I have met. We are truly blessed to live in a nation where those of humble backgrounds can achieve the American dream and give generously of their resources to help future generations.

Supporting Cast

Lieutenant Governor

Robert Anderson, Democrat, Newton, 1983–1987
Jo Ann Zimmerman, Democrat, Van Buren County, 1987–1991
Joy Corning, Republican, Bridgewater, 1991–1999
Kim Reynolds, Republican, Saint Charles, 2011 – current

Chief of Staff

1. David Oman
2. Doug Gross
3. Alan Thoms
4. David Roederer
5. Robert Rafferty
6. Gretchen Tegeler
7. Jeff Boeynik
8. Matt Hench
9. Michael Bousselot

Press Secretary/Communications Director

Susan Neely
Richard Vohs
Christina Martin
Eric Woolson
Timothy Albrecht
Jimmy Centers
Ben Hammes

Schedulers

Bonnie Smalley
Alicia Freed

Executive Assistants
Grace Copley
Margaret Hough

Staff Members
Bob Alles
Royce Anthony
Elizabeth Arndt
Christie Bartel
Steve Berger
Rosalie Blakesley
Carmine Boal
John & Janet Boehm
Barb Brown
Faye Brown-Brewton
Barbara Burnett
Chris Carruthers
Jill Cawiezill
Steven Churchill
Gerd Claybaugh
Nick Crawford
M.J. Dolan
Carol Droste
Carol Duncan
Phil Dunshee
Linda Fandel
Barb Filer
Bobbie Finch
Brenna Findley
Rand Fisher
Darin Fratzke
Tom Gabriel
Katie Gillette
Eric Goranson
Lisa Green
Adam Gregg

Jennifer Harbeson
Almo Hawkins
Keith Heffernan
Laurene Hendricks
Doug Hoelscher
Leo Hough
Kathryn Hove
Dave Hudson
Catherine Huggins
Ann Hughes
Bonita Jansma
Jacob Johnson
Brian Kennedy
Jim Kersten
Jake Ketzner
Jennifer Kingland
Mary Kate Knor
David Kochel
Chuck Larson
Charles Larson
Matt Leopold
Mark Logdson
Dan McConnell
Lynn McRoberts
Lester Menke
Max Miller
Nancy Nelson
Terry Nelson
Jon Neuschwanger
Larry Noble
Sara Opie
Jodi Ott
Bill Pasut
Don Paulin
Dick Ramsey
Jackie Romp

Mary Boote-Roth
Greta Rouse
Vicky Sande
Connie Schmett
Tina Shaw
Linda Shawver
Ron Shortenhaus
Phil Smith
Mark Snell
Phil Stanhope
Stacie Stanley
Greg Steffan
Gary Steinke
Mark Stewart
Jenae Stokesbary
Ted Stopulos
Gail Stutz
Pat Surles
Earl Usher
Blake Waggoner
Erica Weeklund
Caitlin Williams
Josh Wilson
Dan Wolter
Dwight Wright
Carol Zeigler
Anne Zimmerman

Footnotes

1. Terry Branstad interview, State Capitol, Jan. 14, 2014.
2. Ibid.
3. Ruth Leibrand interview, Forest City, Mansion Museum, April 4, 2014.
4. Terry Branstad interview, State Capitol, Jan. 14, 2014.
5. Lyle Simpson interview, Lyle Simpson's office, Des Moines, May 14, 2014.
6. Terry Branstad interview, State Capitol, Jan. 14, 2014.
7. Ibid.
8. Ibid.
9. Ibid.
10. Jack Bender article on Herb Thompson, *Daily Iowan*, Dec. 9, 1949.
11. Terry Branstad interview, drive to Iowa City, Oct. 5, 2013.
12. Herb Thompson interview, by phone, May 5, 2104.
13. Terry Branstad interview, State Capitol, Jan. 14, 2014.
14. Ibid.
15. Jim Redel interview, by phone, May 5, 2014.
16. Ibid.
17. Jerry Tweeten, Forest City, Mansion Museum, April 4, 2014.
18. Terry Branstad interview, State Capitol, Jan. 28, 2014.
19. Ibid.
20. Cindy Monroe interview, by phone, April 7, 2014.
21. Ibid.
22. Sally Prickett interview, by phone, April 8, 2014.
23. Ibid.
24. Terry Branstad interview, State Capitol, May 14, 2014.
25. Conscience of a Conservative, Barry Goldwater, pages 10–11.
26. Ibid., back cover
27. Ibid., page XIX.
28. Ibid., page 16.
29. Ibid., page XIX.
30. Ibid., page 15.
31. Ibid., page IX.
32. Ibid., page IX.
33. Terry Branstad interview, State Capitol, Jan. 14, 2014.
34. Ibid.
35. Ibid.

36. Sally Prickett interview, by phone, April 8, 2014.
37. Ibid.
38. Terry Branstad interview, State Capitol, April 18, 2014.
39. Ibid.
40. Ibid.
41. Lyle Simpson interview, Lyle Simpson's office, May 14, 2014.
42. Terry Branstad interview, State Capitol, April 18, 2014.
43. Ibid.
44. Ibid.
45. Ibid.
46. Richard Johnson interview, by phone, Oct. 15, 2014.
47. Chris Branstad interview, Terrace Hill, Feb. 5, 2014.
48. Ibid.
49. Richard Johnson interview, by phone, Oct. 15, 2014.
50. Chris Branstad interview, Terrace Hill, Feb. 5, 2014.
51. Terry Branstad interview, State Capitol, Jan. 14, 2014.
52. Chris Branstad interview, Terrace Hill, Feb. 5, 2104
53. Terry Branstad interview, State Capitol, Jan. 14, 2014.
54. Ibid.
55. Richard Schwarm interview, by phone, Nov. 3, 2014.
56. Chris Branstad interview, Terrace Hill, Feb. 5, 2014.
57. Terry Branstad interview, State Capitol, Jan. 14, 2014.
58. Chris Branstad interview, Terrace Hill, Feb. 5, 2014.
59. Dan Davis interview at Forest City, Mansion Museum, August 26, 2014.
60. Lyle Simpson interview, Lyle Simpson's office, May 14, 2014.
61. Ibid.
62. Doug Gross interview, Doug Gross's office, Des Moines, Nov. 11, 2014.
63. Lyle Simpson interview, Lyle Simpson's office, Des Moines, May 14, 2014.
64. Randy Smith interview, by phone, March 26, 2015.
65. Ibid.
66. Lyle Simpson interview, Lyle Simpson's office, Des Moines, May 14, 2014.
67. Richard Johnson interview, by phone, Oct. 15, 2014.
68. Article, *Forest City Summit*, Oct. 8, 1981.
69. Chuck Offenburger column, "Iowa Boy," *Des Moines Register*, Nov. 23, 1980.
70. Terry Branstad interview, State Capitol, Jan. 14, 2014.
71. James Strohman, "The Undefeated Governor," *CityView*, Jan. 9–14, 2014, page 14.
72. Article, *Forest City Summit*, March 4, 1982.
73. Lyle Simpson interview, Lyle Simpson's office, Des Moines, June 27, 2014.
74. David Fisher interview, David Fisher's office, Des Moines, Oct. 29, 2014.
75. Ibid.
76. Ibid.
77. Susan Neely interview, e-mail, Jan. 13, 2015.

78. David Fisher interview, David Fisher's office, Des Moines, Oct. 29, 2014.
79. T. Johnson, "Conlin is queried by local students," *Daily Iowan*, Nov. 2, 1982.
80. Ibid.
81. James Strohman, "The Undefeated Governor," *CityView*, Jan. 9–14, 2014, page 14.
82. David Fisher interview, Fisher's office, Des Moines, Oct. 29, 2014.
83. Associated Press (undated story).
84. Associated Press (undated story).
85. Associated Press (undated story).
86. Lyle Simpson interview, Lyle Simpson's office, Des Moines, June 27, 2014.
87. Terry Branstad interview, State Capitol, Jan. 14, 2014.
88. Ibid.
89. Iowa State Lottery website, www.ialottery.com.
90. Ibid.
91. Terry Branstad interview, State Capitol, Jan. 28, 2014.
92. Jeff Stein e-mail, Nov. 11, 2014.
93. David Yepsen, column, *Des Moines Register*, June 15, 1988.
94. Susan Weaver, "A new family settles in at Terrace Hill," *Des Moines Register*, April 3, 1983.
95. *pencer Daily Reporter*, March 11, 1986.
96. Ibid.
97. Iowa Public Television special on the farm crisis, Sept. 6, 2013.
98. Doug Gross interview, Doug Gross's office, Des Moines, Nov. 11, 2014.
99. Kenneth Pins in the *Des Moines Register*, June 27, 1988.
100. *Spencer Daily Reporter*, Oct. 1, 1988.
101. Ibid.
102. Terry Branstad interview, State Capitol, April 18, 2014.
103. Associated Press report, Oct. 30, 1986.
104. Susan Neely e-mail, Jan. 13, 2015.
105. Ibid.
106. *Daily Iowan*, Iowa City, Nov. 5, 1986.
107. Ibid.
108. Ibid.
109. James Strohman, "The Undefeated Governor," *City View*, Jan. 9–14, 2014, page 14.
110. James P. Gannon, "How to fix what's wrong with Iowa," *Des Moines Register*, Oct. 2, 1988
111. Thomas A. Fogarty, "Branstad begins year as chairman of nation's governors," *Des Moines Register*, July 6, 1989.
112. Ibid.
113. Our Views, *Mason City Globe-Gazette*, Sept. 27, 1989.
114. David Yepsen, "Why Branstad is going to win again," *Des Moines Register*, May 30, 1988.
115. Associated Press, April 28, 1988.

116. Kevin Baskins, *Des Moines Register* (date unknown), 1989.
117. Art Cullen, *Forest City Summit*, April 6, 1990.
118. *Spencer Daily Reporter*, April 10, 1990.
119. David Yepsen column, *Des Moines Register*, May 30, 1988.
120. *New York Times*, May 28, 1990.
121. Ibid.
122. *Spencer Daily Reporter*, June 6, 1990.
123. Teachers Union endorsement, *Daily Iowan*, June 11, 1990.
124. Joy Corning interview, by phone, Dec. 13, 2014.
125. Associated Press story, March 25, 1990.
126. David Roederer interview, by phone, Dec. 12, 2014.
127. Terry Branstad interview, State Capitol, April 18, 2014.
128. Associated Press (undated).
129. A letter to Iowans, by Gov. Terry E. Branstad, numerous papers
130. Thomas A. Fogarty, "Branstad adjusts to private life," *Des Moines Register*, May 16, 1999.
131. *Spencer Daily Reporter*, Dec. 15, 1993.
132. *Spencer Daily Reporter*, June 7, 1994.
133. David Yepsen, "On Capitol Hill" column, *Des Moines Register*, Feb. 2, 1994.
134. Mike Glover, "GOP clash proves instructive," Associated Press, Feb. 14, 1994.
135. *Daily Iowan*, May 13, 1994.
136. *Spencer Daily Reporter*, June 1, 1994.
137. *Chicago Tribune*, June 9, 1994.
138. David Fisher interview, David Fisher's office, Des Moines, Oct. 29, 2014.
139. Lyle Simpson interview, Lyle Simpson's office, Des Moines, June 27, 2014.
140. Riley Lewis interview, Mansion Museum, Forest City, Aug. 26, 2014.
141. *Chicago Tribune*, June 9, 1994.
142. Associated Press, Nov. 8, 1994.
143. Ibid.
144. James Strohman, "The Undefeated Governor," *City View*, Jan. 9–14, 2014, page 14.
145. Ibid.
146. Lyle Simpson interview, Lyle Simpson's office, Des Moines, June 27, 2014.
147. Chris Branstad interview, Terrace Hill, Des Moines, Feb. 5, 2014.
148. Terry Branstad speech at GOP Convention, August 1996.
149. Michele Applegate, "Branstad picks Surf for 50th birthday bash," *Mason City Globe-Gazette*, Sept 9, 28, 1996.
150. David Yepsen, "Branstad says this term is his last term," *Des Moines Register*, March 8, 1997.
151. Associated Press article (undated).
152. "Branstad cancels trip to Russia," Associated Press, May 27, 1998.
153. Jonathan Roos, "Governor's salary dwarfed," *Des Moines Register*, March 5, 1995.
154. Ibid.

155. Terry Branstad's final speech, Jan. 17, 1999.
156. Associated Press article, Dec.12, 1998.
157. Doug Gross interview, Doug Gross's office, Des Moines, Nov. 11, 2014.
158. Terry Branstad interview, State Capitol, Jan. 28, 2014.
159. Chris Branstad interview, Terrace Hill, Des Moines, Feb. 5, 2014.
160. Craig Robinson, "The Comeback," *Iowa Republican*, June 26, 2010, page 4.
161. Chris Branstad interview, Terrace Hill, Des Moines, Feb. 5, 2014.
162. Richard Schwarm interview, by phone, Nov. 3, 2014.
163. Ibid.
164. Doug Gross interview, Doug Gross's office, Des Moines, Nov. 11, 2014.
165. Craig Robinson, "The Comeback," *Iowa Republican*, June 26, 2010, page 4.
166. Jeff Boeynik interview, Jeff Boeynik's office, Des Moines, Dec. 29, 2014.
167. Craig Robinson, "The Comeback," *Iowa Republican*, June 26, 2014, page 5.
168. Des Moines Register, Sept. 14, 2010.
169. Ibid.
170. Ibid.
171. *The Gazette*, Cedar Rapids, June 24, 2010.
172. Kim Reynolds interview, by phone, Dec. 13, 2014.
173. Ibid.
174. Associated Press, Nov. 2, 2010.
175. Smart Politics website, http://editions.lib.umn.edu/smartpolitics/2013/04/10/the-top-50-longest-serving-gov/.
176. Ibid.
177. Kathie O'Bradovich, "Conditions good for Branstad bid," *Des Moines Register*, June 8, 2013.
178. Jennifer Jacobs, *Des Moines Register*, Jan. 14, 2014.
179. Kathie O'Bradovich, "Good news, bad news for Branstad in new poll," *Des Moines Register*, March 9, 2014.
180. *Des Moines Register*, Aug. 13, 2014.
181. Ibid.
182. Wikipedia, Nixon trip to China 1972, https://en.wikipedia.org/wiki/1972_Nixon_visit_to_China
183. Jo Ling Kent, NBC, "China's president-in-waiting returns to Iowa," Feb. 15, 2012.
184. Ibid.
185. Ibid.
186. Associated Press, Branstad toast (date unknown).
187. Associated Press, Branstad in China (date unknown).
188. Terry Branstad editorial, *China Daily*, April 16, 2013.
189. Nick Compton column, Voices & Commentary, *Des Moines Register* (date unknown).
190. George C. Ford, *The Gazette*, Cedar Rapids, Dec. 20, 2014.
191. "Trouble at Terrace Hill over tours through governor's mansion," (date and publication unknown).

192. Phoebe Wall Howard, "Governor's house in need of repairs, lawmakers told," *Des Moines Register*, March 14, 1995.
193. Chris Branstad interview, Terrace Hill, Des Moines, Feb. 5, 2014.
194. Ibid.
195. Associated Press article (date unknown).
196. Phoebe Wall Howard, "Running Mates," *Des Moines Register*, Feb. 20, 1994.
197. Ibid.
198. Rob Borsellino column, *Des Moines Register*, Feb. 9, 1999.
199. Thomas A. Fogarty, "14 years and counting," *Des Moines Register*, Dec. 29, 1996.
200. "Gov. Branstad's no stargazer," Associated Press, May 10, 1988.
201. Doug Gross interview, Doug Gross's office, Des Moines, Nov. 11, 2014.
202. Associated Press article, Feb. 19, 1993.
203. Reid Forgrave, "Chris Branstad still doesn't seek spotlight," *Des Moines Register*, Oct. 27, 2010.
204. Chris Branstad interview, Terrace Hill, Des Moines, Feb. 5, 2014.
205. Matt Hinch interview, by phone, Dec. 13, 2014.
206. Ibid.
207. Witnessed by author at Iowa-MSU game, Iowa City, Oct. 5, 2013.
208. Matt Hinch interview, by phone, Dec. 13, 2014.
209. Bill Knapp interview, Bill Knapp's office, Des Moines, Sept. 20, 2013.
210. Henry Tippie interview, by phone, March 5, 2015.
211. Jeff Boeynik interview, Jeff Boeynik's office, Des Moines, Dec. 29, 2014.
212. Mike Glover, "It's time to consider Branstad's legacy," Associated Press, Sept. 22, 1998.
213. Doug Gross interview, Doug Gross's office, Des Moines, Nov. 11, 2014.
214. Susan Neely interview by e-mail, Jan. 13, 2015.
215. Lyle Simpson interview, Lyle Simpson's office, Des Moines, June 27, 2014.
216. *Storm Lake Pilot Tribune*, May 11, 1998.
217. David Yepsen, "Branstad sees opportunity in last office year," *Des Moines Register*, June 27, 1997.
218. Doug Gross interview, Doug Gross's office, Des Moines, Nov. 11, 2014.
219. State Senator Jeff Danielson e-mail sent on Sept. 18, 2014.
220. David Fisher interview, Dave Fisher's office, Des Moines, Oct. 29, 2014.
221. Susan Neely interview by e-mail, Jan. 13, 2015.
222. Joy Corning interview, by phone, Dec. 13, 2014.
223. Kim Reynolds interview, by phone, Dec. 13, 2014.
224. Tim Albrecht interview, by phone, Dec. 17, 2014.
225. Ibid.
226. Jimmy Centers interview in governor's office, State Capitol, Jan. 28, 2015.
227. Susan Neely interview by e-mail, Jan. 13, 2015.
228. Ken Sullivan interview, by phone, Nov. 14, 2014.
229. Doug Gross interview, Doug Gross's office, Des Moines, Nov. 11, 2014.

230. Ken Sullivan interview, by phone, Nov. 14, 2014.
231. David Fisher interview, David Fisher's office, Des Moines, Oct. 29, 2014.
232. Lyle Simpson interview, Lyle Simpson's office, Des Moines, June 27, 2014.
233. Tim Albrecht interview, by phone, Nov. 25, 2014.
234. Chuck Offenburger, "High time for a party," *Des Moines Register*, Jan. 18, 1995.
235. Margaret Hough interview in governor's office, Jan. 28, 2014.
236. Ibid.
237. Ibid.
238. Leo Hough interview in State Capitol, Jan. 28, 2014.
239. Margaret Hough interview in governor's office, Jan. 28, 2014.
240. Lyle Simpson interview, Lyle Simpson's office, Des Moines, June 27, 2014.
241. Ibid.
242. Henry Tippie interview, by phone, March 15, 2014.
243. Terry Branstad interview, State Capitol, Sept. 12, 2014.
244. Matt Hinch interview, by phone, Dec. 13, 2014.
245. *The Real Deal: The Life of Bill Knapp*, William B. Fredericks, BPC, Des Moines, 2013, page 212.
246. Terry Branstad interview, governor's office, State Capitol, Sept. 12, 2014.
247. Margaret Hough interview in governor's office, Jan. 28, 2014.
248. Terry Branstad interview, governor's office, State Capitol, Sept. 12, 2014.
249. David Roederer interview, by phone, Dec. 12, 2014.
250. Jonathan Roos, "Branstad relishes his role as salesman for the state," *Des Moines Register*, Oct. 7, 1990.
251. Thomas A. Fogarty, "14 years as governor and counting," *Des Moines Register*, Dec. 29, 1996.
252. Doug Gross interview, Doug Gross's office, Des Moines, Nov. 11, 2014.
253. Dennis Ryerson column, "What will be Branstad's legacy," *Des Moines Register*, 1991 (date unknown).
254. Bonnie Smalley interview, by phone, March 27, 2015.
255. Jeff Stein e-mail, Nov. 11, 2014.
256. Jonathan Roos, "Branstad set for finale," *Des Moines Register*, Jan. 14, 1998.
257. Tim Albrecht interview, by phone, Nov. 25, 2014.
258. Terry Branstad interview, State Capitol, Sept. 12, 2014.
259. Craig Robinson, *Iowa Republican*, Aug. 30, 2013.
260. Kim Reynolds interview by phone, Dec. 13, 2014.
261. Richard Doak, "Iowa's Greatest Governors: The Best led US in Change," *Des Moines Sunday Register*, July 7, 2013, page 19P.
262. *Lincoln and the Union Governors*, 2013, Southern Illinois University Press
263. Ibid.
264. Ibid.
265. Ibid.
266. Richard Doak, "Iowa's Greatest Governors: The Best led US in Change," *Des Moines*

Sunday Register, July 7, 2013, page 19P.

267. Ibid.
268. https://en.wikipedia.org/wiki/William_L._Harding
269. Richard Doak, "Iowa's Greatest Governors: The Best led US in Change," *Des Moines Sunday Register*, July 7, 2013, page 19P.
270. Ibid.
271. *The Real Deal: The Life of Bill Knapp*, William B. Fredericks, BPC, Des Moines, 2013, page 153.

Interview Subjects

Terry Branstad
Chris Branstad
Margaret Hough
Leo Hough
Lyle Simpson
Doug Gross
Tim Albrecht
Ruth Leibrand
Jerry Tweeten
Cindy Monroe
Sally Prickett
Herb Thompson
Jim Redel
Richard Johnson
Richard Schwarm
Dan Davis
Randy Smith
David Fisher
Susan Neely
Jeff Stein
Joy Corning
David Roederer
Riley Lewis
Bill Knapp
Jeff Boeynik
Kim Reynolds
Matt Hinch
Jimmy Centers
Henry Tippie
Ken Sullivan
Bonnie Smalley

Sources

Many newspaper and magazine articles were read, from these publications and organizations: The Associated Press, Des Moines Register, Daily Iowan (Iowa City), Forest City Summit, Mason City Globe-Gazette, City View (Des Moines), The Gazette (Cedar Rapids), Spencer Daily Reporter, Storm Lake Pilot Tribune, New York Times, Chicago Tribune, China Daily, and The Iowa Republican. The following web sites were consulted: Smart Politics and Iowa Lottery, as well as Wikipedia, and one Iowa Public Television program. A special thank you goes to the Mansion Museum in Forest City, which houses hundreds of newspaper and magazine articles, many of them unmarked and not dated, covering the life and career of Terry Branstad.

In addition, over 30 interviews were conducted and the following books were consulted:

1. *Conscious of a Conservative*, by Barry Goldwater, 1990, Regnery Gateway, Inc., Washington, D.C.
2. *George Clinton, Master Builder of the Empire State*, by John K. Lee, 2010, Syracuse University Press, Syracuse, New York.
3. *Lincoln and the Union Governors*, by William C. Harris, 2013, Southern Illinois University Press, Carbondale, Illinois.
4. *The Real Deal: The Life of Bill Knapp*, by William B. Friedricks, 2013, Business Publications Corporation, Inc., Des Moines.

Index

Throughout this index, the abbreviation TB will be used to indicate references to Terry Branstad. Page numbers appearing in italic type refer to pages that contain photographs.